W9-DGM-890

The Rich Get Richer
and the Poor Get Prison

Ideology, Class, and Criminal Justice

i

*I see no reason why big shot crooks should
go free while the poor ones go to jail.*

Jimmy Carter

The Rich Get Richer and the Poor Get Prison

Ideology, Class, and Criminal Justice

Jeffrey H. Reiman

School of Justice
The American University
Washington, D.C.

JOHN WILEY & SONS

New York · Chichester · Brisbane · Toronto · Singapore

Library of Congress Cataloging in Publication Data
Reiman, Jeffrey H
   The rich get richer and the poor get prison.

   Includes index.
   1. Criminal justice, Administration of—United States.

I. Title.
HV8138.R42   364′.973   78-23986
ISBN 0-471-04726-0

Printed in the United States of America

10 9 8 7 6

iv

For Sue

Credits

Preface

It is obvious that the American criminal justice system is failing in the war against crime, and equally obvious that American criminal justice policies often contribute to the very problem that they seek to solve. This book is an attempt to understand this failure: its dimensions, its mechanisms, its causes, and its moral implications.

It is today a commonplace of social analysis, as in the past it was a tenet of common sense, that if social practices endure, they must—even the most blatantly irrational of social practices—be serving some interests. With this as a starting point, I determine if there are any interests that might be served by the continuing failure of the American criminal justice system. I try to see if there is an angle from which this failure is a success, and find indeed that there is.

To understand this conclusion, it is necessary to see that the failure of the criminal justice system to protect us is not haphazard. It has a pattern. The criminal justice system devotes the lion's share of its crime-fighting resources to fighting against crimes like murder and mugging, crimes that are characteristically committed by the poor in our society. And, although our prisons are filled with poor criminals, little dent is made in the overall volume of their crimes. Indeed, there is reason to believe that prisons serve more as training grounds for future criminality than for good citizenship. But this failure of the system to stem the crimes of the poor must be viewed in the context of another and more easily overlooked failure: the failure to fight vigorously, moreover often the failure even to treat as criminal, the dangerous acts of the wealthy and powerful. We have a system shaped by economic bias from the start. The dangerous acts and crimes unique to the wealthy are either ignored or treated lightly, while for the so-called common crimes, the poor are far more likely than the well-off to be arrested, if arrested charged, if charged convicted, and if convicted sentenced to prison. Hence, the failure of the criminal justice system has a pattern: *the rich get richer and the poor get prison.*

But failure is in the eye of the beholder. This failure *succeeds* in conveying to the general public a message of enormous ideological value to those at the top in our society: the message that the greatest danger to the average citizen comes from below him or her on the economic ladder, not from above. For those at the top, this failure is a success.

No one who writes a book can be mindless of the power of words. In our own times, we have rightly been made conscious of the power of technically neutral nouns like "man" and pronouns like "he" to convey a picture of a world in which the actors are all male. Not only is this a distortion of the world in which we live, it is a link in the chain that bars women from full and active participation in social, economic, and political life. In this book I have therefore striven to avoid the use of words that are technically neutral but are effectively masculine. In a few instances, however, I use the masculine form even though the reference is to men and women. My reasoning is this. There are other evils in the world to be remedied besides sexism. The injustices visited on our fellow human beings in the name of criminal justice are among the gravest of these evils. This book is offered in the hope of contributing to the reduction of these evils. Only rarely, where there was no way to eliminate traditional masculine nouns or pronouns without weakening the force of what I consider to be an important statement, do I let the traditional forms stand. Readers may find my judgments here faulty but I hope they will accept my reasons.

Jeffrey H. Reiman

Acknowledgments

This book is the product of seven years of teaching in the School of Justice (formerly, the Center for the Administration of Justice), a multidisciplinary criminal justice education program at The American University in Washington, D.C. I have had the benefit of the school's lively and diverse faculty and student body. And, although they will surely not agree with all that I have to say, I have drawn heavily on what I have learned from my colleagues over the years and stand in their debt. In addition, more than is ordinarily recognized, a teacher receives guidance from students as they test, confirm, reject, and expand what they learn in class in the light of their own experience. Here, too, I am deeply in debt. My thanks go to the hundreds of students who have shared some part of their world with me as they passed through The American University, and in particular to three students whose encouragement, loyalty, and wisdom are very much a part of the development of the ideas in this book: Elizabeth Crimi, Bernard Demczuk, and Lloyd Raines.

I express my gratitude to The American University for providing me with a summer research grant that enabled me to devote full time to the book in the summer of 1976, when most of the actual writing was done. I am also grateful to Bernard Demczuk who was my research assistant during the academic year 1975 to 76, and who gathered much of the research data. I owe thanks as well to Cathy Sacks for ably and carefully typing the final manuscript.

Drafts of the manuscript for this book were read in whole or in part by (or at) Bernard Demczuk, Sue Hollis, Richard Myren, Lloyd Raines, Phillip Scribner, I. F. Stone, and John

Wildeman. I am grateful for their many comments and I incorporate many of their recommendations in the final version. I have made my mistakes in spite of them.

Finally, for teaching me about artichokes, the meaning of history, and countless other mysteries, this book is dedicated to Sue Headlee Hollis.

J. H. R.

Contents

The Rich Get Richer and the Poor Get Prison

Ideology, Class, and Criminal Justice

Introduction

Criminal Justice Through the Looking Glass, or Winning by Losing

The inescapable conclusion is that society secretly wants *crime,* needs *crime, and gains definite satisfactions from the present mishandling of it.*

Karl Menninger, *The Crime of Punishment*

A criminal justice system is a mirror in which a whole society can see the darker outlines of its face. Our ideas of justice and evil take on visible form in it, and thus we see ourselves in deep relief. Step through this looking glass to view the American criminal justice system—and ultimately the whole society it reflects—from a radically different angle of vision.

In particular, entertain the idea that the goal of our criminal justice system is not to reduce crime or to achieve justice but to project to the American public a visible image of the threat of crime. To do this, it must maintain the existence of a sizable or growing population of criminals. And to do this, it must fail in the struggle to reduce crime.

You will rightly demand to know how and why a society such as ours would tolerate a criminal justice system "designed to fail" in the fight against crime. Indeed, a consider-

1

able portion of this book is devoted to showing how the failure of the criminal justice system serves the interests of the powerful in America. Right now, however, a short explanation of how this upside-down idea of criminal justice was born will best introduce it and myself.

Last year I taught a seminar for graduate students, entitled The Philosophy of Punishment and Rehabilitation. Many of the students were already working in the field of corrections as probation officers or prison guards or half-way-house counselors. First we examined the various philosophical justifications for legal punishment, and then we directed our attention to the functioning of the actual correctional system. For much of the semester we talked about the myriad inconsistencies and cruelties and overall irrationality of the system. We discussed the arbitrariness with which offenders are sentenced to prison and the arbitrariness with which they are treated in prison. We discussed the lack of privacy and the deprivation of sources of personal identity and dignity, the ever-present physical violence, as well as the lack of meaningful counseling or job training within prison walls. We discussed the harassment of parolees, the inescapability of the "ex-con" stigma, the refusal of society to let a person finish paying his or her "debt to society," and the near-total absence of meaningful noncriminal opportunities for the ex-prisoner. We confronted time and again the bald irrationality of a society that builds prisons to prevent crime knowing full well that they do not, a society that does not even seriously try to rid its prisons and post-release practices of those features that guarantee a high rate of *recidivism:* the return to crime by prison alumni. How could we fail so miserably? We are neither an evil nor a stupid nor an impoverished people. How could we continue to bend our energies and spend our hard-earned tax dollars on cures we know are not working?

Toward the end of the semester I put before the students an idea that appears from time to time in the literature of sociology: Imagine that instead of designing a correctional system to reduce and prevent crime, we had to design one that would maintain and encourage the existence of a stable and visible "class" of criminals. What would it look like? The response was electrifying. In briefer and somewhat more orderly form, here is a sample of the proposals that emerged in our discussion:

First. It would be helpful to have a number of irrational laws on the books, such as laws against heroin or prostitution or gambling—laws that prohibit acts that have no clear victim and that really do not prevent the acts they make illegal. This would make many people "criminals" for what they regard as normal behavior and would increase their need to engage in *secondary* crime (the drug addict's need to steal to pay for drugs, the protitute's need for a pimp, since police protection is unavailable, etc.).

Second. It would be good to give police, prosecutors, and judges broad discretion to decide who got arrested, who got charged, and who got sentenced to prison. This would mean that almost anyone who got as far as prison would know of others who committed the same crime but who either were not arrested or were not charged or were not sentenced to prison. This would assure us that a good portion of the prison population would experience their confinement as arbitrary and unjust and thus respond with rage, which would make them more "antisocial," rather than with remorse, which would make them feel more bound by social norms.

Third. The prison experience should be not only painful but also demeaning. The pain of loss of liberty might deter future crime. But demeaning and emasculating prisoners by placing them in an enforced childhood characterized by no privacy and no control over their time and actions, as well as by the constant threat of rape or assault, is sure to overcome any deterrent effect by weakening whatever capacities a prisoner had for self-control.

Fourth. It goes almost without saying that prisoners should neither be trained in a marketable skill nor provided with a job after release. And, of course, their prison records should stand as a perpetual stigma to discourage employers

from hiring them. Otherwise, they might be tempted *not* to
return to crime after release.

Fifth. The ex-offenders' sense that they can never pay their
debt to society, that they will always be different from
"decent citizens," should be reinforced by the following
means. They should be deprived for the rest of their lives of
rights, such as the right to vote. They should be harassed by
police as "likely suspects" and be subject to the whims of
parole officers who can at any time threaten to send them
back to prison for things no ordinary citizens could be arrested for, such as going out of town or drinking or frater-
nizing with the "wrong people."

And so on.

In short, *asked to design a system that would maintain
and encourage the existence of a stable and visible "class
of criminals," we "constructed" the American criminal
justice system!*

What is to be made of this? First, it is, of course, only part
of the truth. Some prison officials do try to treat their inmates
with dignity and to respect their privacy and self-determina-
tion to the greatest extent possible within an institution
dedicated to involuntary confinement. Minimum security
prisons and halfway houses are certainly moves in this direction. Some prisons do provide meaningful job training, and
some parole officers are not only fair but go out of their way
to help their "clients" find jobs and make it "legally." And,
of course, plenty of people are arrested for doing things that
no society ought to tolerate, such as rape, murder, assault, or
armed robbery, and many are in prison who might be preying on their fellow citizens if they were not. *All of this is
true.* Complex social practices are just that: *complex.* They
are neither all good nor all bad. But for all that, the "suc-
cesses" of the system, the "good" prisons, the halfway
houses that really help offenders make it are still the exceptions. They are not even prevalent enough to be called the
beginning of the trend of the future. *On the whole, most of the
system's practices make more sense if we look at them as in-*

gredients in an attempt to maintain rather than to reduce crime!

This statement calls for an explanation. The one I will offer is that the system does this in order to keep before the public the *real* threat of crime and the *distorted* image that crime is primarily the work of the poor. The value of this *to those in positions of power* is that it deflects the discontent and potential hostility of middle America away from the classes above them and toward the classes below them. If this explanation is hard to swallow, it should be noted in its favor that it not only explains our dismal failure to reduce crime, but it also explains why the criminal justice system functions in a way that is biased against the poor at every stage from arrest to conviction. Indeed, even at the earlier stage, when crimes are defined in law, the system primarily concentrates on the predatory acts of the poor and tends to exclude or deemphasize the equally or more dangerous predatory acts of those who are well off. In sum, I will argue that *the criminal justice system fails to reduce crime while making it look like crime is the work of the poor.* And it does this in a way that conveys the image that the real danger to decent, law-abiding Americans comes from below them, rather than from above them, on the economic ladder. This image sanctifies the status quo with its disparities of wealth, privilege, and opportunity and thus serves the interests of the rich and powerful in America—the very ones who could change criminal justice policy if they were really unhappy with it.

Therefore, it seems appropriate to ask you to look at criminal justice "through the looking glass." On one hand, this suggests a reversal of common expectations. Reverse your expectations about criminal justice and entertain the notion that the system's real goal is the very reverse of its announced goal. On the other hand, the figure of the looking glass suggests the prevalence of image over reality. Indeed, my argument is that the system functions the way it does *in order to create a particular image of crime: the image that it is a threat from the poor.* Of course, for this image to be

believable there must be a reality to back it up. The system
must actually fight crime—or at least some crime—but only
enough to keep it from getting out of hand and to keep the
struggle against crime vividly and dramatically in the
public's view—never enough to reduce or eliminate crime. I
call this way of looking at criminal justice policy the *Pyrrhic
defeat* theory.

I claim no particular originality for the Pyrrhic defeat
theory. It is a child of the marriage of several streams of
western social theory. And although this will be discussed at
greater length in what follows, it will serve clarity to indicate
from the start the parents and the grandparents of this child.
The idea that crime serves important functions for a society
comes from Emile Durkheim. The notion that public policy
can best be understood as serving the interests of the rich
and powerful in a society stems from Karl Marx. From Kai
Erikson is derived the notion that the institutions that are
designed to fight crime serve instead to contribute to its existence. And from Richard Quinney comes the concept of the
"reality" of crime as *created* in the process that runs from the
definition of some acts as "criminal" in the law to the treatment of some persons as "criminals" by the agents of the
law. The Pyrrhic defeat theory combines these ideas into the
view that the failure of criminal justice policy becomes intelligible when we see that it creates the "reality" of crime as the
work of the poor and thus projects an image that serves the
interests of the rich and powerful in American society.

The Pyrrhic defeat theory veers away from traditional
Marxist accounts of legal institutions insofar as such accounts generally emphasize the *repressive* function of the
criminal justice system, while my view emphasizes its *ideological* function. On the whole, Marxists see the criminal
justice system as serving the powerful by *successfully* repressing the poor. My view is that the system serves the
powerful by its *failure* to reduce crime, not by its success.
Needless to add, insofar as the system fails in some respects
and succeeds in others, these approaches are not necessarily
incompatible. Nevertheless, it is important to keep in mind

that in looking at the ideological rather than the repressive function of criminal justice, I shall focus primarily on the image its *failure* conveys rather than on what it actually *succeeds* in repressing. To these remarks should be added the recognition that since the 1960s, a new generation of Marxist theorists, primarily French, has begun to look specifically at the ideological functions performed by the institutions of the state. Most noteworthy in this respect, is the work of Louis Althusser and Nicos Poulantzas.[1]

Having located the Pyrrhic defeat theory in its family tree, a word about the relationship between crime and economics is in order. It is my view that the social order (shaped decisively by the economic system) causes or promotes most of the crime that troubles us. This is true of all classes in the society, since a competitive economy that refuses to guarantee its members a decent living places pressures on all members to enhance their economic position by whatever means available. *Nevertheless*, these economic pressures work with particular harshness on the poor, since their condition of extreme need and their relative lack of access to opportunities for lawful economic advancement vastly intensify for them the pressures toward crime that exist at all levels of our society.

These views lead to others that, if not taken in their proper context, may strike you as paradoxical. Evidence will be presented showing that there is a considerable amount of crime in our society at all socioeconomic levels. At the same time, it will be argued that poverty is a *source* of crime—I say "source" rather than "cause" because the link between poverty and crime is not like a physical relationship between cause and effect. Many, perhaps most, poor people do not commit crimes. Nevertheless, there is evidence suggesting that the particular pressures of poverty lead poor people to commit a higher proportion of the crimes that people fear (such as homicide, burglary, and assault) than their number in the population. There is no contradiction between this and the recognition that those who are well off commit many more crimes than is generally acknowledged, both of the sort widely feared and of the sort not widely feared (such as "white collar" crimes). There is no contradiction here, because, as will be shown, the poor are arrested far more frequently than those who are well off when they have committed the same crimes; and the well-to-do are almost never arrested for white collar crimes. Thus, if arrest records were brought in line with the real incidence of crime, it is likely that those who are well off would appear in the records far more than they do at present, even though the poor would still probably figure disproportionately in arrests for the crimes people fear. In addition to this, it will be argued that those who are well off commit acts that are not defined as crimes and yet that are as harmful or more so than the crimes people fear. Thus, if we had an accurate picture of who is really dangerous to society, there is reason to believe that those who are well off would receive still greater representation. On this basis, the following propositions will be put forth, which may appear paradoxical if these various levels of analysis are not kept distinct.

1.   Society fails to protect people from the crimes they fear by (among other things, documented in Chapter 1) refusing to alleviate the poverty that breeds them.
2.   The criminal justice system fails to protect people from the most serious of dangers by failing to define the dangerous acts of those who are well off as crimes (documented in Chapter 2), and by failing to enforce the law vigorously against the well-to-do when they commit crimes (documented in Chapter 3).
3.   By virtue of these and other failures, the criminal justice system succeeds in creating the image that crime is almost exclusively the work of the poor, an image that serves the interests of the powerful (argued in Chapter 4).

The view that the social order is responsible for crime does not mean that individuals are wholly blameless for their criminal acts or that we ought not have a criminal justice system able to protect us against them. To borrow an anal-

ogy from Ernest van den Haag, it would be foolhardy to
refuse to fight a fire because its causes were suspect. The
fact that society produces criminals is no reason to avoid
facing the realization that the criminals it produces are dangerous and must be dealt with. Also, although blaming
society for crime may require that we tone down our blame of
individual criminals, it does not require that we deny entirely
that they are responsible for their crimes. This is particularly
important to keep in mind in view of the fact that so many of
the victims of the crimes of the poor are poor themselves. To
point to the unique social pressures that cause the poor to
prey on one another is to point to a mitigating, not an excus-
ing, factor. Even the victims of exploitation and oppression
have moral obligations not to harm those who do not exploit
them or who share their oppression.

Footnotes

1. See especially, Louis Althusser, "Ideology and Ideological State
   Apparatuses," in *Lenin and Philosophy and Other Essays* (London: New Left Books, 1971), pp. 121-173; and Nicos Poulantzas,
   Fascism and Dictatorship (London: New Left Books, 1974), pp.
   299-309. These writers refer back to the pioneering insights of
   Antonio Gramsci into the ideological functions of state institu-
   tions. See Quintin Hoare and Geoffrey Nowell-Smith, eds., *Selec-
   tions from the Prison Notebooks of Antonio Gramsci* (London:
   Lawrence and Wishart, 1971); and Carl Boggs, *Gramsci's Marxism* (London: Pluto Press, 1976). For other contemporary analy-
   ses of the relationship between the state and ideology, see Ralph
   Miliband, *The State in Capitalist Society* (New York: Basic
   Books, 1969), pp. 179-264; and Jürgen Habermas, *Legitimation
   Crisis* (Boston: Beacon Press, 1975). The Frankfurt School of
   social theory, of which Jürgen Habermas and Herbert Marcuse
   are probably the best known representatives, is distinguished by
   the application of Marxian as well as Freudian theory to the
   analysis of ideology. See Martin Jay, *The Dialectical Imagination: The Frankfurt School of Critical Theory, 1930-1950* (Boston:
   Little, Brown, 1973).

1

Crime Control in America: Nothing Succeeds Like Failure

My love she speaks softly
She knows there's no success like failure
And that failure's no success at all.

Bob Dylan, *Love Minus Zero/No Limit*

a. Designed to Fail

Something in the American grain keeps us from admitting defeat both to ourselves and to others. Perhaps it is the heady air of the long-closed frontier trapped in our lungs; whatever it is, it keeps us from confessing to anything more serious than the temporary elusiveness of victory. Americans never confess to having lost a war, although we do admit there are a few we did not win. And domestically, no public policy ever fails, although some do not succeed. Hence President Ford's remarks about crime control in America can only be read as a confession of failure, *American style*:

> ... America has been far from successful in dealing with the sort of crime that obsesses America day and night—I mean street crime, crime that invades our neighborhoods and our homes—murders, robberies, rapes, muggings, holdups, break-ins—the kind of brutal violence that makes us fearful of strangers and afraid to go out at night.[1]

11

Of course, we do not need a presidential announcement to
know that our assaults on the crime problem are a failure
anymore than we need a presidential announcement to know
that Monday follows Sunday. Everyone knows that for all
our efforts, intelligence, and money, serious crime is not even
leveling off. It is increasing at rates that leave our other
increasing headaches, such as overpopulation and inflation,
far behind. Indeed, President Ford's remarks themselves no
more than hint at the enduring and abysmal nature of our
failure. In that same message, Mr. Ford said:

> Ever since the first presidential message on crime, in 1965,
> strenuous Federal efforts, as well as State and local initiatives,
> have been undertaken to reduce the incidence of crime in the
> United States. Yet, throughout this period, crime has continued
> to increase. Indeed the Federal Bureau of Investigation's latest
> estimates are that the rate of serious crime—murder, forcible
> rape, robbery, aggravated assault, burglary, larceny and auto
> theft— was 17 percent higher in 1974 than in 1973. *This is the
> largest increase in the 44 years the Bureau has been collecting
> statistics.*
> Since 1960, although billions of dollars have been spent on
> law enforcement programs, the crime rate has more than
> doubled. Moreover, *these figures reflect only the reported
> crimes.* A study of unreported crime sponsored by the Law
> Enforcement Assistance Administration indicates that *the
> actual level of crime in some cities is three to five times greater
> than that reported.*[2]

In 1960 the average citizen had less than a 1-in-50 chance
of being a victim of one of the crimes on the FBI Index. In
1974, a citizen had nearly a 1-in-20 chance of being victimized,
and in 1976, a 1-in-19 chance.[3]* In other words, speaking
roughly, if crime had leveled off at the 1960 rate, on the
average, each citizen could expect to be a victim of an Index
Crime (murder, forcible rape, robbery, aggravated assault,
burglary, larceny, or auto theft) once in 50 years, or a little
over one time during his or her life. At the 1976 rate, the
average citizen can expect to be a victim of a serious crime

about once in 20 years, or between three and four times during his or her life. And this is only if crime levels off at the 1976 rate, without taking into consideration the extent of unreported crime that does not get into the FBI accounting system. Taking unreported crime into account and projecting ahead, if crime rates continue to increase as they have over recent years, it is not unreasonable to suggest that within the decade, we face the likelihood of living in a society in which, on the average, each citizen is the victim of a serious crime every five years or less!

How are we to comprehend this monstrous failure? It appears that our government is failing to fulfill the most fundamental task of governance: keeping our streets and homes safe, ensuring us of what the Founding Fathers called "domestic tranquility," providing us with the minimal requirement of civilized society. It appears that our *new centurions* with all their modern equipment and know-how are no more able than the old Roman centurions to hold the line against the forces of barbarism and chaos. How are we to understand this failure?

---

*In general the national crime statistics used in this book are from the FBI's *Uniform Crime Reports: Crime in the United States, 1974* (see footnotes for full references). I have kept to this even though subsequent reports have been issued while this book was being prepared for publication. There are two reasons for this. First, later reports generally continue the trends identified in the *UCR-1974* with little alteration. *UCR-1976* shows the rate of Index Crimes per 100,000 inhabitants rising dramatically from 4850.4 in 1974 to 5281.7 in 1975 and then falling slightly to 5266.4 in 1976. Second, the statistics for 1974 are roughly contemporary with other statistics used in this book, such as those for harm produced by noncriminal acts, and thus give a more accurate view of the comparative danger of crime. Where appropriate, I have included the statistics for 1976 in the text or in the footnotes at the end of each chapter. Also, in this paragraph, I have translated an annual 1-in-50 chance of victimization into an expectation of victimization once in 50 years and an annual 1-in-20 chance into an expectation of victimization once in 20 years, purely to illustrate the change in the magnitude of the crime threat. Technically, an annual 1-in-20 or 1-in-50 chance works out to approximately a 64% chance of victimization in 20 or 50 years, respectively.

One way, of course, is to look at the *excuses* that are offered for the failure. And this we will do—but mainly to show that they do not hold up! In general, these excuses fall into two categories. Some apologists point to some feature of modern life, such as urbanization or population growth (particularly the rapid increase in the number of individuals in the crime-prone ages of 15 to 24), and they say that this feature is responsible for the growth in crime. This means that crime cannot be reduced unless we are prepared to return to horse-and-buggy days or to abolish adolescence. *Translation*: We are failing to reduce crime because it is impossible to reduce crime.

The second batch of excuses takes the form of arguing that we simply do not know how to reduce crime. *Translation*: Even though we are doing our best, we are failing to reduce crime because our knowledge of the causes of crime is still too primitive to make our best good enough.

These excuses simply do not pass muster. Although increasing urbanization and a growing youth population account for some of the increase in crime, they by no means account for all the increase, and certainly not for the impossibility of reducing crime. Crime rates vary widely (and wildly) when we compare cities of similar population size and density. Some very large and densely populated cities have lower crime rates than small and sparse ones. Some cities are high in one type of crime and low in another, and so on. What this means is that growing crime is not a simple, unavoidable consequence of increasing urbanization. If crime rates vary between large cities, urbanization cannot explain away our inability to reduce crime *at least* to *the lowest* rates prevalent in large cities. Similarly, the crime rate has increased far more rapidly than the youth population has both in absolute numbers and as a fraction of the total population. This means that growing crime is not a simple, unavoidable consequence of a growing youth population. If crime rates are increasing faster than the young themselves are, then increasing youth itself is not the cause of increasing crime. We have to know why 15- to 24-year-old young people are committing more crimes now than they did in the past, and it is no answer to point to their youth. Growing youth population cannot explain away our inability to reduce crime *at least* down to the rate at which the young are increasing in our population.

On the other hand, the excuse that we do not know how to reduce crime also does not hold up. The bald truth is that we *do* know some of the sources of crime and *we obstinately refuse to remedy them*! We know that poverty increases the pressures to commit crimes in pursuit of property and that crimes to obtain property account for about 90 percent of the crime rate—and yet we do little to improve the conditions of our impoverished inner-city neighborhoods beyond clicking our tongues over the strange coincidence that these are also the neighborhoods with the highest crime rates. We know that our prisons undermine human dignity and that the "ex-con" stigma closes the door to many lawful occupations—and yet we do little to improve these conditions beyond shaking our heads over the fact that so much crime is committed by *recidivists*: people who have already enjoyed the hospitality of our jails and penitentiaries. We know that heroin addiction "forces" people into crime *because* of the high prices of illegal heroin—and yet we refuse to make cheap heroin legally available. We know that guns figure in most murders and make possible many thefts—and yet we refuse to adopt effective gun control. In other words, we may not know how to eliminate crime, but we certainly know how to reduce crime and the suffering it produces. The simple truth is that, as with crime so with crime reduction, *ignorance is no excuse*.

Since the excuses do not explain our failure to reduce crime, we are back at square one. The question "How shall we comprehend this monstrous failure?" still stares us in the face. Examining the excuses has been of little avail. Indeed, it has produced a result opposite from the one hoped for. It has suggested that our failure is an avoidable one. What has to be explained is not why we *cannot* reduce crime *but why we will not*! Oddly enough, this paradoxical result points us in the direction of an answer to our question.

Failure is, after all, in the eye of the beholder. The last runner across the finish line has failed in the race only if he or she wanted to win. If the runner wanted to lose, the "failure" is, in fact, a success. Here, I think, lies the key to understanding our criminal justice system.

If we look at the system as "wanting" to reduce crime, it is an abysmal failure—and we cannot understand it. If we look at it as *not* "wanting" to reduce crime, it a howling success—and all we need to understand is why the goal of the criminal justice system is to fail to reduce crime. If we can understand this, then the system's "failure," as well as its obstinate refusal to implement the policies that could remedy that "failure," becomes perfectly understandable.

In other words, I propose that we can make more sense out of criminal justice policy by assuming that its goal is to maintain crime than by assuming that its goal is to reduce crime!

I call this outrageous way of looking at criminal justice policy the *Pyrrhic defeat* theory. A "Pyrrhic victory" is one in which a military victory is purchased at such a cost in troops and treasure that it amounts to a defeat. The Pyrrhic defeat theory argues that the failure of the criminal justice system yields such benefits to those in positions of power that it amounts to success. In what follows, I will try to explain the failure of the criminal justice system to reduce crime by showing the benefits that accrue to the powerful in America from this failure. I will argue that from the standpoint of those with the power to make criminal justice policy in America: *Nothing succeeds like failure.* And I challenge you to keep an open mind and determine for yourself whether or not the Pyrrhic defeat thesis does not make more sense out of criminal justice policy and practice than the old-fashioned idea that the goal of the system is to reduce crime.

The Pyrrhic defeat thesis has several components. Above all, it must provide an explanation of *how* the failure to reduce crime could benefit anyone—anyone other than criminals, that is. This task is addressed in Chapter 4, which is entitled "To the Vanquished Belong the Spoils: Who Is Winning the Losing War Against Crime?" I argue there that the failure to reduce crime broadcasts a powerful *ideological* message to the American people, a message that benefits and protects the powerful and privileged in our society by legitimating the present social order with its disparities of wealth and privilege and by diverting public discontent and opposition away from the rich and powerful and onto the poor and powerless.

To provide this benefit, however, not just any failure will do. It is necessary that the failure of the criminal justice system take a particular shape. *It must take a dive in the fight against crime while making it look like serious crime and thus the real danger to society is the work of the poor.* Indeed, the system accomplishes this both by what is does and by what it refuses to do. In Chapter 2, "A Crime by Any Other Name," I argue that the criminal justice system refuses to label and treat as crime a large number of acts that produce as much or more damage to life and limb as the so-called crimes of the poor. In Chapter 3, "The Rich Get Richer and the Poor Get Prison," I show how, even among the acts that are treated as crimes, the criminal justice system is biased from start to finish in a way that guarantees that *for the same crimes* members of the lower classes are much more likely than members of the middle and upper classes to be arrested, convicted, and imprisoned—thus providing living "proof" that crime is a threat from the poor. (A statement of the seven main propositions that form the core of the Pyrrhic defeat theory is found in Chapter 2, Section c.)

It is important to recognize that the argument in Chapters 1 through 4 does not amount to a conspiracy theory. I do not believe that our law makers refuse to legalize heroin or implement gun control or improve our prisons out of a conscious intention to allow crime to flourish. I do not believe that a governor ever vetoes a piece of legislation, thinking "Well, I can't let that pass, it might really reduce crime." All that the Pyrrhic defeat theory requires us to believe is the following. On one hand, those who are most victimized by crime are not those in positions to make and implement policy. Crime falls more frequently and more harshly on the poor than on those who are better off (see Chapter 4). On the other hand, there are enough benefits to the wealthy from the identification of crime with the poor and the system's failure to reduce crime (see Chapter 4, section b) that those with the power to make profound changes in the system feel no compulsion nor see any incentive in making them. When I speak of the criminal justice system as "designed to fail," I mean no more than this.

In Chapter 5, I present in dialogue form an argument that the conditions described in Chapters 1, 2, and 3 (whether or not one accepts my explanation for them in Chapter 4) have the effect of undermining the essential moral difference between criminal justice and crime itself. In this chapter, called "Criminal *Justice* or *Criminal* Justice: A Matter of Moral Conviction," I make some recommendations for re- form of the system. However, these are not offered as ways to "improve" the system but as the minimal conditions neces- sary to establish the moral superiority of that system to crime itself!

In the remainder of the present chapter, I explore in some detail the excuses for the failure to reduce crime and show that they will not suffice. In addition, I offer evidence to back up my assertion that there are policies that could reduce crime which we refuse to implement. I then briefly outline the relationship between the Pyrrhic defeat theory and the criminological theory of Kai Erikson and Emile Durkheim, from which several of its basic concepts are derived.

b. Three Excuses That Will Not Wash, or How We Could Reduce Crime If We Wanted To

On July 23, 1965, President Lyndon Johnson signed an Executive Order establishing the President's Commission on Law Enforcement and Administration of Justice to investigate the causes and nature of crime, to collect existing knowledge about our criminal justice system, and to make recommendations about how that system might better meet "the challenge of crime in a free society." The commission presented its report to the president early in 1967, thick with data and recommendations. Since we are a nation higher on commissions than on commitments, it should come as no surprise that for all the light cast on the crime problem by the President's Commission, little heat has been generated and virtually no profound changes in criminal justice policy have taken place in the ten years since the report was issued.

During this period, however, more and more money has been poured into crime control with the bleak results I have already outlined. When the commission wrote, it estimated that over $4 billion was being spent annually—at the national, state, and local levels to pay for police, courts, and correction facilities in the fight against crime.[4] Since that time the total number of reported Index Crimes grew from 4,710,800 in 1965 to a staggering 11,304,800 in 1976![5] The total cost to the public for this brand of domestic tranquility reached $12,985,155,000 for fiscal year 1972-1973, with over a million persons employed by the criminal justice system, 623,606 of them providing "police protection."[6] Needless to say, dollar-for-dollar, crime control is hardly an impressive investment.

Nevertheless, multiplying almost as fast as crime and anticrime dollars are excuses for our failure to stem the rapid growth of crime (not to say the failure to actually reduce it) in the face of increased expenditure, personnel, research, and data. Three excuses (or, more charitably, "explanations") have sufficient currency to make them worthy of consideration as well as to set in relief the Pyrrhic defeat thesis, which I propose in their place:

1. First Excuse

One excuse is that crime is an inescapable companion of any complex, populous, industrialized society. As we become more complex, more populous, more industrialized, and particularly more *urbanized*, we will have more crime as inevitably as we will have more ulcers and more traffic. These are the costs of modern life, the benefits of which abound and clearly outweigh the costs. Growing crime then takes its place alongside death and taxes. We can fight it, but we cannot win, and we should not tear our hair out about it.

It takes little reflection to see that this is less an explanation than a recipe for resignation. Furthermore, it does not account for the fact that other complex, populous, and highly industrialized nations such as Japan and West Germany have crime rates that are not only lower than ours but that do not accelerate as quickly as ours and even occasionally decrease. In 1971, the total number of criminal offenses known to the police in Japan was 1,244,168, a little more than 1000 offenses for every 100,000 inhabitants. In other words, about *one-fifth* the number of serious offenses known to the police in America that year occurred in a country with *half* the population of the United States crowded onto a land less than *one-twentieth* the size of the United States. More striking, however, is that while American crime was soaring in the 1970s, Japan reports that offenses known to the police decreased to 1,191,549 in 1973. West Germany reports a decline in the per capita rate of all known crimes from 55 per thousand in 1947 to 30 per thousand in 1955.[7]

Moreover, the "costs of modern life" or urbanization excuse does not account for the striking differences in the crime rates *within* our own modern, complex, populous, and urbanized nation. Within the United States, the homicide rate ranges from 1.4 per 100,000 inhabitants in North Dakota to 17.8 in Georgia.[8] Discussing the homicide rate in a 1968 issue, *Time* magazine reported that "in some Northern ghettos it hits 90, just as it did some years ago in the King murder city of Memphis. Texas, home of the shoot-out and divorce-by-pistol, leads the U.S. with about 1,000 homicides a year, more than 14 other states combined. Houston is the U.S. murder capital: 244 last year, more than in England, which has 45 million more people."[9] By 1974, however, Texas was in third place behind California and New York, which reported 1985 and 1913 murders and nonnegligent man-slaughters, respectively, as compared to Texas's mere 1646—and Houston's glory as the murder capital had clearly faded. Houston reported 330 in 1974, roundly outdone by Los Angeles with 481 and Chicago with 970 and left far behind by New York City, which captured the 1974 murder title with an astounding 1554![10]

And such variations are not limited to murder. A comparison of crime rates (incidence of FBI Index Crimes per 100,000 inhabitants) for standard metropolitan statistical areas (areas "made up of a core city with a population of 50,000 or more inhabitants and the surrounding county or counties which share certain metropolitan characteristics") reveals a striking *lack* of correlation between crime rate and population size (which we can take as a reasonable, though rough, index of urbanization and the other marks of modernity, such as complexity and industrialization, that are offered as explanations for the intractabililty of crime). Citizens of the New York City metropolitan area (population 9,826,130) have about *the same chance* of being victimized by an Index Crime (6072.2 per 100,000) as citizens living in and around Battle Creek, Michigan, where the population is 181,846 and the crime rate is 6052.9. A New Yorker is, on the other hand, *half as likely* as a citizen of the Phoenix, Arizona area to be a victim of a property crime and *twice as likely* to be a victim of a violent crime, since the property crime rate around Phoenix is 9141.8 (compared to New York's 4764.6) and the violent crime rate is 653.5 (compared to New York's 1307.5). The Phoenix metropolitan area (population 1,173,300) has the highest crime rate for any standard metropolitan statistical area in the nation—about twice the national crime rate. For 1974, the FBI reports a crime rate of 9795.3 per 100,000 residents of the Phoenix area, proving that Arizona may not be as good for your health as the ads claim.[11]

There is, of course, no denying that crime becomes more of a problem once we reach cities with populations of over 50,000 or 100,000 persons. However, this is about all that can be said. If crime were an unavoidable and intractable consequence of urbanization, we should expect crime rates to be higher wherever population or population density (number of persons per square mile) is higher. But the facts do not bear this out. Instead, they indicate a striking *lack of correlation* between a city's crime rate and its population or population density (see Table 1).[12]

In other words, classifying crime with death and taxes and saying that it is an inevitable companion of modernity or urbanization just will not explain our failure to reduce it. Even if death and taxes are inevitable (although unfortunately not in that order), some die prematurely and some die suspiciously and some pay too much in taxes and some pay none at all. And none of these variations is inevitable or unimportant. So too with crime. Even if crime is inevitable in modern societies, its rates and types vary extensively—and this is neither inevitable nor unimportant. Indeed, the variations in crime rates between modern cities and nations is proof that the *extent* of crime is not a simple consequence of urbanization. Other factors must explain the differences. And it is these differences that suggest that although some crime may be an ineradicable consequence of urbanization, this in no way excuses our failure to reduce crime at least to the lowest rates reported in modern cities and nations.

2. Second Excuse

A second excuse takes the form of attributing the growth in crime to young people—particularly young men between the ages of 15 and 24. This "explanation" goes as follows: Young people in our society, especially males, find themselves emerging from the security of childhood into the frightening chaos of adult responsibility. Little is or can be done by the adult society to ease the transition by providing meaningful outlets for the newly bursting youthful energy aroused in still immature and irresponsible youngsters. Hence, these youngsters both mimic the power of manhood and attack the society that frightens and ignores them by resorting to

Table 1 Metropolitan Areas Ranked by ... Population and Crime Rate

Standard Metropolitan Statistical Areas by Population	Overall Crime Rate (Ranking by total number FBI Index Crimes per 100,000 persons)	Violent Crime Rate (Ranking by number of FBI Index Violent Crimes per 100,000 persons)	Property Crime Rate (Ranking by number of FBI Index Property Crimes per 100,000 persons)
New York City (9,826,130)	5th (6072.2)	1st (1307.5)	8th (4764.6)
Chicago (7,071,400)	6th (5965.9)	4th (793.9)	7th (5171.9)
Los Angeles (6,964,946)	4th (6992.1)	3rd (890.4)	4th (6101.8)
Detroit (4,465,102)	2nd (7383.0)	2nd (949.0)	3rd (6434.0)
Washington, D.C. (3,038,567)	7th (5940.3)	5th (687.2)	5th (5253.0)
Pittsburgh (2,353,674)	10th (2934.8)	9th (313.3)	10th (2621.6)
Milwaukee (1,421,968)	9th (4164.1)	10th (226.1)	9th (3938.0)
Denver (1,395,846)	3rd (7321.2)	7th (538.5)	2nd (6782.8)
Phoenix (1,173,700)	1st (9795.3)	6th (653.5)	1st (9141.8)
Indianapolis (1,139,189)	8th (5632.5)	8th (451.5)	6th (5181.1)

Source: Federal Bureau of Investigation, *Uniform Crime Reports-1974.*

23

violent crime. Add to this the rapid increase of people in this age group since the baby boom of the 1940s, and we have another explanation that amounts to a recipe for resignation: We can no more expect to reduce crime than we can hope to eradicate adolescence. We can fight crime, but it will be with us until we figure out a way for people to get from childhood to adulthood without passing through their teens.

There can be no doubt that youngsters show up disproportionately in arrest figures. In 1965, persons between the ages of 11 and 24 constituted 23.4 percent of the nation's population. They represented, however, 50 percent of those arrested for willful homicide, rape, robbery, and aggravated assault; and a staggering 75.2 percent of those arrested for larceny, burglary, and motor vehicle thefts.[13] Using more recent statistics, *Time* reports that "forty-four percent of the nation's murderers are 25 or younger, and 10 percent are under 18. Of those arrested for street crimes, excluding murder, fully 75 percent are under 25 and 45 percent are under 18."[14]

However, there are many problems with this "explanation." First and most obvious is that the crime rate is growing much faster than either the absolute number of young people or their percentage of the population. Neither the number nor the percentage of youngsters has doubled between 1965 and 1971, although serious crime has. Nor has the number or percentage of teenagers jumped 17 percent between 1973 and 1974, although serious crime has.

From 1960 to 1974, the number of Americans aged 15 to 24 climbed from 24.5 million to 39.5 million, an increase of about 60 percent. As a fraction of the total population, they increased about 50 percent, from 13.6 percent to 18.7 percent of the total populace. Neither figure comes close to explaining the fact that reported crimes *tripled* in that same period, going from 3,360,000 in 1960 to over 10,000,000 in 1974. Neither figure comes close to explaining the fact that the number of youngsters aged 15 to 24 who were arrested also *tripled* in that same period.[15] In other words, there is every reason to suspect that both the overall volume of crime and the number of crimes committed by 15- to 24-year-olds is

increasing at a much faster rate than the number of youngsters in this age bracket is increasing.

The meaning of these statistics is clear: our failure to stem
the growth in crime cannot be explained away by pointing to
the growth in the number of young people. If crime is
increasing faster than the youth population, then that
increase cannot be explained by the increase in youths. If
crime *among* these youngsters is increasing, then this
certainly is not explained by their youth. In neither case does
the increase in young people provide an excuse for failing to
reduce the growth of crime at least to the rate at which the
number of young people is growing. So another excuse for our
failure fails to excuse.

3. *Third Excuse*

The third excuse is the hardest to swallow. This excuse, in
its crudest form, is that we simply are not yet smart enough
to solve the problem. We have tried and continue to try in
good faith, but we can only go as far as our own lights, and
they have not yet lit the path to the solution of the crime
problem. In differing forms and in differing degrees of
despair, this excuse is proffered by experts—both academic
and professional—in the various divisions of the criminal
justice system. An article by Joel D. Weisman, entitled
"Chicago Reflects Police Frustration in Fight Against
Crime," in the *Washington Post* gives a good sampling of
this view among experts on the police:

> There is controversy over whether police departments can
> significantly affect crime. Boston Police Commissioner Robert
> J. diGrazia claims police can only displace crime—not reduce
> or eliminate it. "It's like squeezing a balloon," said [David]
> Fogel [executive director of the Illinois Law Enforcement
> Commission]. "You push the air away from where you're
> squeezing but it expands the rest of the balloon."
>
> James Q. Wilson, a professor of political science at Harvard
> University and author of the book *Thinking About Crime*, said

police can contribute to reducing crime but it is unclear by how much. The data is too unreliable, he contended.

"All those answers the sociologists had for us in the 1960s aren't so definite now," said [Franklin] Zimring [head of the University of Chicago's Center for Studies in Criminal Justice]. "For that matter, all of the law enforcement answers weren't so right either."[16]

An article by Leroy Aarons, also in the *Washington Post*, entitled, "U.S. Penal System 'Truths' Questioned," reflects similar bewilderment among correctional officials. Reporting the conclusions of a "recent issue of *Corrections* magazine," which "devoted 27 pages to an article on the current ferment in the field," Aarons writes:

The article concluded, based on interviews with wardens, administrators and students of corrections around the country that:

• There is little or no evidence that correctional "treatment" programs work.
• The gradual restructuring of the correctional system over the last 50 years around the notion of individualized and enforced treatment for all offenders was a mistake.
• A radically new approach is needed that will provide both better protection for the public and a more realistic view of what can and cannot be done to cut recidivism, the return to criminal behavior.

"What the new approach should include is a matter of dispute," the article said.

Aarons concludes his own article with an observation drawn from current doubts among corrections experts but applicable to the whole criminal justice system:

It seems clear that, in the long run, solutions to the age-old problem of what to do with those individuals deemed law-breakers still elude society.[17]

This excuse says, in short, that growing crime is not inherently intractable, as is claimed by the partisans of excuses one and two—but it might as well be. It might as well be because we simply do not know what to do about it. And so we fail, and we cannot be blamed for our failure.

To believe this excuse, you must believe the following: That the United States, with virtually limitless resources, capable of spending hundreds of billions of dollars to fight a hardly believable "threat" in Vietnam, cannot summon the resources and will to do battle with a threat that haunts almost everyone in our society and makes them fearful to walk the streets and hardly more secure at home; that the United States, with technology and information beyond the dreams of any previous generation, indeed any previous civilization, capable of placing a human being on the moon and a heart in a human being, cannot figure out at least *some* of the causes of some crime and eliminate those causes; and that the United States, with over a million law enforcement and criminal justice personnel, with training and literally billions of work-hours of experience in the "fight against crime," has not developed the expertise even to dent the rising crime rate much less actually to reduce it. This is just too much to swallow.

But there is more. There are, in fact, things that we do know about the sources of crime. Note that I have said "sources" rather than "causes," because the kind of knowledge we have is far from the precise knowledge that a physicist has about how some event *causes* another. We know that poverty, slums, and unemployment are *sources* of street crime. We do not know if (or how) they *cause* crime, because we know as well that many, if not most, poor, unemployed slumdwellers do not engage in street crime. And yet to say that this means we do not *know* that such conditions increase the likelihood of an individual resorting to violent crime is like saying that we do not *know* that a bullet in the head is deadly because some people survive or because we do not fully understand the physiological process that links the wound with the termination of life.

Those 15- to 24-year-olds who figure so prominently in arrest statistics are not drawn equally from all economic strata. Although there is much reported and even more

unreported crime among middle-class youngsters, the street
crime that is attributed to this age group and that makes our
city streets a perpetual war zone is largely the work of poor
ghetto youth. This is the group at the lowest end of the
economic spectrum. This is a group among whom unemployment approaches 50 percent with underemployment (the rate
of persons either jobless or with part-time low-wage jobs) still
higher. This is a group with no realistic chance (for any but a
rare individual) to enter college or amass sufficient capital
(legally) to start a business or to get into the union-protected,
high-wage, skilled-job markets. This much we do know, just
as we know that of the over 1 million persons processed
through the criminal justice system on any given day, fully
80 percent come from the lowest 15 percent of the economic
spectrum.[18] We know that poverty is a *source* of crime, even if
we do not know how it *causes* crime—and yet we do virtually
nothing to improve the life chances of the vast majority of
the inner-city poor. They are as poor as ever and are facing
cuts in welfare and other services. They are as unemployed
as ever and are inevitably the ones to go when recession
leads to layoffs. Their housing is as rundown as ever, and
they face the continual and growing threat of forced removal
from their neighborhoods in the name of "urban renewal."

There are other things we know as well. We know that
prison produces more criminals than it cures. We know that
more than 70 percent of the inmates in the nation's prisons or
jails are not there for the first time. We know that prison
inmates are denied autonomy and privacy and subjected to
violence and that they are stripped of every possiblity to
control their lives and thus of any basis for self-respect. As a
result, they are bereft of both training and reason to control
their lives on the outside. And once on the outside, rarely
trained in a marketable skill and burdened with the stigma
of a prison record, few opportunities for noncriminal employment are open to them. Should we then really pretend that we
do not *know* why they turn to crime? Can we honestly act as
if we do not know that our prison system (combined with our
failure to ensure the ex-con of a meaningful post-release
noncriminal alternative) is a *source* of crime? Recidivism

does not happen because ex-cons miss their alma mater. In fact, if prisons are built to deter people from crime, one would expect that ex-prisoners would be most deterred because the deprivations of prison are more real to them than to the rest of us. Recidivism is thus a doubly poignant testimony to the job that prison does in preparing its graduates for crime— and yet we do little to change the nature of prisons or to provide real services to ex-convicts.

We know that it is about as difficult to obtain a handgun in the United States as a candy bar. We know that there are more than 100 million guns in private use in this country. In 1968 Franklin Zimring tried to estimate the numbers of guns in civilian hands by using both the results of public opinion polls and the available figures on domestic production, as well as foreign import of firearms for civilian use. He concluded that:

> Survey results thus indicate ownership of approximately 80 million firearms, while production and import totals indicate approximately 100 million. We can do no better than average these two figures and *conservatively* estimate the number of firearms now in civilian hands in this country . . . 35 million rifles, 31 million shotguns, and *24 million handguns*—in 60 million households.[19]

More recently, speaking before the Law Enforcement Executives Narcotics Conference, Attorney General Edward Levi, estimated that the number of handguns in the United States is over 40 million "and that the number increases each year by 2.5 million."[20] The President's Crime Commission reported that in 1965, "5,600 murders, 34,700 aggravated assaults and the vast majority of the 68,400 armed robberies were committed by means of firearms. All but 10 of 278 law enforcement officers murdered during the period 1960-65 were killed with firearms." The commission concluded almost a decade ago that

> more than one-half of all willful homicides and armed robberies, and almost one-fifth of all aggravated assaults, involve use of firearms. *As long as there is no effective gun-control legisla-*

*tion, violent crimes and the injuries they inflict will be harder
to reduce than they might otherwise be.*[21]

The situation has worsened since the commission's warning. The FBI's annual report on crime in the United States for 1974 indicates "that almost 10 of every 100,000 Americans were murdered last year [1974], 4 percent more than in 1973," and the "68 percent of the homicides were committed through the use of firearms and 54 percent were committed with handguns."[22]

In the face of all these alarming trends, President Ford declared in his message to Congress of June 19, 1975: "I am unalterably opposed to Federal registration of guns or the licensing of gun owners. I will oppose any effort to impose such requirements as a matter of Federal policy." And this was said in a message that the president described to reporters as "a special message spelling out in concrete terms the program for curbing crime and insuring 'domestic tranquility'."! Since America is a nation of free movement over statelines, gun control *must* be tackled at the federal level to have any significant impact at all—this has already been confirmed by the experience of states that have enacted strict gun-control legislation. Hence, to oppose gun control as a matter of federal policy is simply to oppose effective gun control!

Can we believe that a president sincerely wants to cut down on violent crime and the injuries it produces when he opposes even as much as *registering* guns or *licensing* gun owners, much less actually restricting the sale and movement of guns as a matter of national policy? Are we to believe that the availability of guns does not contribute to our soaring crime rate? Zimring's study indicates that areas with a high number of privately owned guns have more crimes involving guns than do areas with lower numbers of privately owned firearms. His data also indicate that cities that experience an increase in legal gun sales also experience an increase in gun-related suicides, accidents, and crimes.[23]

But this is hardly more than common sense would lead us to expect. Can we really believe that if guns were less readily

available, violent criminals would simply switch to other
weapons to commit the same amount of crimes and do the
same amount of damage? Is there a weapon other than the
handgun that works as quickly, that allows it user so safe a
distance, or that makes the criminal's physical strength (or
speed or courage for that matter) as irrelevant? Could a bank
robber hold a row of tellers at bay with a switchblade? Would
an escaping felon protect himself from a pursuing police
officer with a hand grenade? In fact, Zimring's studies also
indicate that if gun users switched to the next deadliest
weapon—the knife—and attempted the same number of
crimes, we could still expect *80 percent fewer fatalities*, since
the fatality rate of the knife is roughly one-fifth that of the
gun. In other words, if guns were eliminated, even if crimes
were not reduced, we could expect to save as many as four out
of every five persons who are now the victims of firearm
homicide!

Finally, the United States has a massive heroin-addiction
problem. The number of users is hard to estimate because we
only know the ones who get caught and because there are a
large but indeterminate number of individuals who (contrary
to popular mythology) shoot up occasionally without becom-
ing addicts—a practice known as "chipping." Nevertheless,
some reasonable methods of arriving at a ballpark estimate
of the number of addicts—that is, regular users who have
developed a physical need for heroin and who therefore
experience painful withdrawal symptoms if they do not shoot
up regularly—have been concocted, and the most conservative figure that emerges is 250,000, with estimates ranging as
high as 600,000![24]

As shocking as this statistic may be, it must be at least as
shocking to discover that there is precious little evidence
proving that heroin is a *dangerous* drug. There is no evidence
conclusively establishing a link between heroin and disease
or tissue degeneration such as that which has been established for tobacco and alcohol. On the basis of the scientific
evidence available, there is every reason to suspect that we
do our bodies more damage, more *irreversible* damage, by

smoking cigarettes and drinking liquor. Most of the physical damage that is associated with heroin use is probably attributable to the trauma of withdrawal—and this, of course, is a product not so much of heroin but of its unavailability.

It might be said that the evil of heroin lies in the fact that it is *addicting*, since this is a bad thing even if the addicting substance is not itself harmful.[25] It it hard to deny that the image of a person enslaved to a chemical is rather ugly and is repugnant to our sense that the dignity of human beings lies in their capacity to control their destinies. More questionable however, is whether this is, in the case of adults, anybody's business but their own. But even so, suppose we agree that addiction is an evil worthy of prevention. Doesn't that make us hypocrites? What about all our other addictions? What about nicotine addiction, which is, like heroin, a physical need the body develops for a chemical that, unlike heroin, we know contributes to cancer and heart disease? What about the 9 or 10 million alcoholics in the nation who are working their way through their livers and into their graves? And what about the people who cannot get started without a caffein fix in the morning, and those who, once started, cannot slow down without their alcohol fix in the evening? Are they not addicts? Suffice it to say, then, at the very least, our attitudes about heroin are inconsistent and irrational, although there is reason to believe they are outrageous and hypocritical. But even if this were not so, even if we could be much more certain that heroin addiction was a disease worth preventing, the fact would remain that the "cure" we have chosen is worse than the disease. We *know* that treating the possession of heroin as a criminal offense produces more crime than it prevents.

In its report entitled *Social Cost of Drug Abuse*, the Special Action Office for Drug Abuse Prevention uses recent figures on the average cost per day of a heroin habit to estimate the amount of theft that heroin addicts must engage in to support their habits. They compute a variety of totals using a combination of different assumptions and then average them to produce their final estimate. They assume that the average addict must supply his or her habit 255 days a year, allowing some time for being in jail or in the hospital; that they must resort to crime to obtain funds for between 33 and 60 percent of their drug needs; and that they must steal three times the dollar value they need, since they must convert their booty into cash through a fence. They assume, then, that there are between 250,000 and 600,000 addicts, who must steal to supply between 33 and 60 percent of habits costing between $43 and $51.50 per day. Using eight combinations of these assumptions, they calculate eight totals reflecting the combination of the lowest to the combination of the highest assumptions. Their totals range from a low of $2.7 billion to a high of $14.2 billion. They drop the lowest two and the highest two as unrealistic in both directions and then compute the average of the middle four:

> The average cost of these alternatives is $6.3 billion, which we shall use as an approximation of cost due to theft related to heroin use.[26]

These figures should be seen in relation to the total dollar value of stolen property across the nation for the same period. In the *Uniform Crime Reports* for 1974, the FBI sets the value of stolen property at $2.6 billion, although this is based on the reports of criminal justice agencies representing areas in which about three-quarters of the nation's population lives.[27] *But even if we double this figure, it is still less than the amount we can reasonably expect addicts to have to steal to support their habits*! Even if we assume that the FBI estimates of the value of stolen property would increase dramatically if we knew the value of unreported theft, we cannot escape the conclusion that theft by heroin addicts—who have no other means of supporting their habits—accounts for an astounding amount of property crime!

And it is essential to recognize that it is not the "disease" of heroin addiction that leads to property crime. This "disease" could be treated with heroin that could be legally produced at a cost of a few cents for a day's supply. Instead, it is the "cure" that leads to property crime. *It is our steadfast refusal to provide heroin through legal sources that, for approximately a quarter of a million individuals on the streets, translates a physical need for a drug into a physical need to steal over $6,000,000,000 worth of property a year!*

Prior to 1914, when anyone could go into a drugstore and purchase heroin and other opiates the way we buy aspirin today, hundreds of thousands of upstanding law-abiding citizens were hooked.[28] Opiate addiction is not in itself a *cause* of crime—if anything, it is a pacifier.[29] However, once sale or possession of heroin is a serious criminal offense, a number of consequences follow. First, since those who supply it face grave penalties, they charge wildly high prices to make the risk worthwhile. And since those who need it face grave pains of withdrawal and have no alternative source, they pay the wildly high prices. What an addict pays even $50 a day for could be produced and sold legally for pennies (as is the case in Great Britain, where heroin is dispensed to addicts by government-controlled clinics). Second, since the supply (and the quality) of the drug fluctuates depending on how vigorously the agents of the law try to prevent it, the addict's life is continuously unstable. Addicts live in constant uncertainty about the next fix and must devote much of their wit and energy to getting it and to getting enough money to pay for it. They do not, then, fit easily into the routines of a 9-to-5 job even if they could get one that would pay enough to support their habits. Finally, all of this adds up to an incentive to be not merely a user of heroin but a dealer as well, since this both earns money and makes one's own supply more certain. Addicts thus have an incentive to find and encourage new addicts that they would not have if heroin were legally and cheaply available. If we add to this the fact that heroin addiction has rapidly increased in spite of all our law enforcement efforts, can we doubt that the cure is worse than the disease? Can we doubt that the cure is a *source* of crime?

In the face of all this, it is hard to believe that we do not know how to reduce crime at all. It is hard not to share the frustration expressed by Norval Morris, dean of the University of Chicago Law School: "It is trite but it remains true that the main causes of crime are social and economic. The question arises whether people really care. The solutions are so obvious. *It's almost as if America wished for a high crime rate.*"[30]

In summary, then, American criminal justice has failed to reduce crime. The failure cannot be excused by claiming that our growing crime problem is intractable or impossible to solve. The failure cannot be excused by claiming that we do not know what to do to reduce crime. Both of these excuses fly in the face of the obvious fact that the crime rate varies under different social conditions and that there are some things we really do know about reducing crime. The second excuse also asks us to believe that the makers of criminal justice policy are more ignorant than we can possibly imagine. Therefore, if a solution is possible and we know it and we can institute it and we do not, what are we left to believe? It must be that we do not want to "solve" the crime problem, or at least some people who are strategically placed do not want to. And if this is so, the *the system's failure is only in the eye of the victim: for those in control, it is a roaring success!*

c. The Joys of Crime: Erikson and Durkheim

Kai T. Erikson, professor of sociology at Yale University, has suggested in his book *Wayward Puritans* that societies derive benefit from the existence of crime and thus there is reason to believe that social institutions work to maintain rather than to eliminate crime. Since the Pyrrhic defeat theory draws heavily upon this insight, it will serve to clarify my own view if we compare it with Erikson's.

Professor Erikson's theory takes as its point of departure the view of crime that finds expression in one of the classic books on sociological theory, *The Division of Labor in Society* by Emile Durkheim. Writing toward the end of the nineteenth century, Durkheim "had suggested that crime

(and by extension other forms of deviation) may actually
perform a needed service to society by drawing people
together in a common posture of anger and indignation. The
deviant individual violates rules of conduct which the rest of
the community holds in high respect; and when these people
come together to express their outrage over the offense and to
bear witness against the offender, they develop a tighter
bond of solidarity than existed earlier."[31]

The solidarity that holds a community together, on this
view, is a function of the intensity with which the members of
the community share a living sense of the group's cultural
identity, of the boundary between acceptable and unacceptable behavior that gives the group its distinctive nature. It is
necessary, then, for the existence of a community *as a
community* that its members learn and constantly relearn
the location of its "boundaries." And, writes Erikson, these
boundaries are learned in dramatic confrontations with

> policing agents whose special business it is to guard the
> cultural integrity of the community. Whether these confronta-
> tions take the form of criminal trials, excommunication hear-
> ings, courts-martial, or even case conferences, they act as
> boundary-maintaining devices in the sense that they demon-
> strate to whatever audience is concerned where the line is
> drawn between behavior that belongs in the special universe of
> the group and behavior that does not.[32]

In brief, this means not only that a community makes good
use of unacceptable behavior *but that it positively needs
unacceptable behavior*. It needs unacceptable behavior not
only to cast in relief the terrain of behavior acceptable to the
community but also to reinforce the intensity with which the
members of the community identify that terrain as their
shared territory. On this view, *deviant behavior is an
ingredient in the glue that holds a community together*.
"This," Erikson continues,

> raises a delicate theoretical issue. If we grant that human
> groups often derive benefit from deviant behavior, can we then

assume that they are organized in such a way as to promote this resource? Can we assume, in other words, *that forces operate in the social structure to recruit offenders and to commit them to long periods of service in the deviant ranks?*...

Looking at the matter from a long-range historical perspective, it is fair to conclude that prisons have done a conspicuously poor job of reforming the convicts placed in their custody; but the very consistency of this failure may have a peculiar logic of its own. Perhaps we find it difficult to change the worst of our penal practices because we *expect* the prison to harden the inmate's commitment to deviant forms of behavior and draw him more deeply into the deviant ranks.[33]

In other words, based on Durkheim's recognition that societies benefit from the existence of deviants, Erikson entertains the view that societies have institutions whose unannounced function is to recruit and maintain a reliable supply of deviants. Modified for our purposes, Erikson's view would become the hypothesis that the American criminal justice system fails to reduce crime because a visible criminal population is essential to maintaining the "boundaries" that mark the cultural identity of American society and to maintaining the solidarity between those who share that identity. In other words, in its failure, the criminal justice system succeeds in providing some of the cement necessary to hold American society together as a society. But since the benefits of deviance are at such an immeasurable and general level as "social solidarity," nothing more than some form—*any* form—of crime-reduction failure is required. This means that the *particular* form in which that failure is taking place in American society is unexplained by the Erikson-Durkheim theory. That is, even if we assume that the existence of deviance serves the purpose of reinforcing the group's boundaries, we do not know why the boundaries are being set where they are, and thus we cannot understand the *particular* form our failure at crime reduction has taken. Other questions float in the wake of this one.

Why have we failed not merely to stem crime, but *particularly* to stem the street crimes of the poor and suite crimes of the rich? Why have we failed in such different ways to reduce these two forms of predatory behavior? Why have we not merely failed but failed miserably? And why have we not merely failed miserably but failed increasingly? Such questions—aimed at eliciting an *explanation* of the *particular form* of the failure of American criminal justice—receive none but the most abstract answers from the Erikson-Durkheim theory, because the need for social solidarity is satisfied by any deviance visible enough to set the boundaries of American society in relief.

None of this should detract from the fact that my view that the failure of the criminal justice system serves dominant social interests is heavily indebted to the theoretical insights of Erikson and Durkheim. By adding to these insights, some of which have their source in Marxist social theory, I will try to show that this failure serves a more specific goal than the necessarily vague one of social solidarity and thus that the specific shape of this failure can be given a more precise explanation than the Erikson-Durkheim theory provides. As I have already suggested, I will argue that the sytem fails *in the way it does* because, in so doing, it broadcasts an ideological message—a message that sanctifies the present social order and thus serves and secures the interests of the powerful and privileged in that social order. Erikson's view gives no adequate answer to the question of why we are failing at crime control *in the way that we are*, since any way of identifying deviants will satisfy the need for social solidarity. I will try to show that the Pyrrhic defeat thesis can provide an answer to this question.

* * *

In this chapter, I have tried to demonstrate that the failure of the criminal justice system is avoidable and cannot be written off as the result of ignorance or impossibility of solution. We must now look at how the system is structured so that this failure takes the shape it does—*a shape that broadcasts the message that the threat of crime and of danger is a threat from the poor.* In Chapter 2, I will show

how our very definitions of serious crime largely exclude from view the dangerous acts of those who are well off. And in Chapter 3, I will show how at every level of the criminal justice system, from arrest to imprisonment, economic bias works to make it more likely that a poor person will end up behind bars than a wealthier person who has committed the same offense.

Abbreviations Used in the Footnotes

Challenge	*The Challenge of Crime in a Free Society: A Report by the President's Commission on Law Enforcement and Administration of Justice* (Washington, D.C.: U.S. Government Printing Office, February 1967).
UCR-1974	Federal Bureau of Investigation, *Uniform Crime Reports for the United States: 1974* (Washington, D.C.: U.S. Government Printing Office, 1975). References to other editions of this annual report will be indicated by *UCR* followed by the year for which the statistics are reported. In general, these reports are published in the fall of the year following the year they cover.
Black Population in the U.S.	U.S. Bureau of the Census, Current Population Reports, Special Studies, Series P-23, No. 54 *The Social and Economic Status of the Black Population in the United States, 1974* (Washington, D.C.: U.S. Government Printing Office, 1975).
Sourcebook	U.S. Law Enforcement Assistance Administration, National Criminal Justice Information and Statistics Service, *Sourcebook of Criminal Justice Statistics - 1974*, by Michael J. Hindelang, Christopher S. Dunn, Alison L. Aumick, and L. Paul Sutton (Washington, D.C.: U.S. Government Printing Office, 1975).

Footnotes

1. *The President's Special Message to Congress on Crime,* June 19, 1975.
2. Ibid. (Emphasis added.)
3. As hard as it may be to believe, the picture painted by the *FBI Uniform Crime Reports,* released November 17, 1975, with statistics through 1974, is even worse than the president's speech indicated. For the period 1960-1974, during which the president said the crime rate "more than doubled," *it in fact increased 2.57 times,* from a rate of 1875.8 Index Crimes per 100,000 inhabitants in 1960 to a rate of 4821.4 Index Crimes per 100,000 inhabitants in 1974. The *UCR* for 1976 reports yet another rise, to 5266.4 Index Crimes per 100,000 inhabitants in that year. Keep in mind that the crime rate is not simply the total volume of crime. It is the volume of crime *in proportion to* the population. The crime rate indicates the citizen's chances of being a victim of one of the crimes on the FBI Index, that is, murder (including nonnegligent manslaughter), forcible rape, robbery, aggravated assault, burglary, larceny, and motor vehicle theft. The crime rates just quoted reflect *all* the crimes on the FBI Index, both violent crimes and property crimes. Violent crimes (murder, rape, robbery, and assault), however, are increasing at a faster pace than property crimes (burglary and the two categories of theft) and thus at a faster pace than the Index as a whole. The rate of victimization by crimes of violence nearly tripled during the period 1960-1974, from a rate of 160 per 100,000 inhabitants in 1960 to a rate of 458.8 in 1974. Among violent crimes, robbery leads the pack, with an increase of three and one-half times from a 1960 rate of 60 per 100,000 persons to a 1974 rate of 208.8. Not far behind it, is forcible rape, probably the most underreported of the violent crimes, with an increase from 9.5 reported rapes per 100,000 in 1960 to a rate of 26.1 in 1974.
4. *Challenge,* p. 35.
5. *UCR-1976,* p. 35; and *UCR-1974,* p. 55.
6. U.S. Law Enforcement Assistance Administration and U.S. Bureau of the Census, *Expenditure and Employment Data for the Criminal Justice System: 1972-73* (Washington, D.C.: U.S. Government Printing Office, 1975), p. 17.
7. The American University, Washington, D.C., Foreign Area Studies Division, *Area Handbook for Japan* (published 1974),

pp. 78, 574; and *Area Handbook for West Germany* (published 1964), p. 608.

8. *UCR-1974*, pp. 63, 68. By 1976, Alabama had taken the lead at 15.1, and Georgia fell behind to 13.9. North Dakota was still at the bottom with 1.4. *UCR-1976*, pp. 38-43.

9. Quoted in *Violence: An Element of American Life*, eds. K. Taylor and F. Soady (Boston: Holbrook Press, 1972), p. 49.

10. *UCR-1974*, pp. 60, 56, 130, 93, 100, 118. In 1976, New York was still comfortably in the lead with 1622 murders, with Chicago the closest challenger, reporting only 814. *UCR-1976*, pp. 84, 105.

11. *UCR-1974*, pp. 3-4, 74, 85.

12. Table 1 further illustrates the *lack* of correlation between city size and crime rates. Five large metropolitan areas (population over 3 million) and five middle-sized metropolitan areas (population between 1,000,000 and 1,500,000) are listed in order of population, from largest to smallest. Each of these is then numerically ranked (in comparison to the others) by overall crime rate, violent crime rate, and property crime rate. Keep in mind that the ranking is by crime *rate* (i.e., incidence of crime per 100,000 inhabitants), not total volume of crime. If crime were a simple function of population size, we would expect the same crime *rate* for all urban areas, and thus no ranking would be possible. If soaring crime is a product of modernization, social complexity, industrialization, urbanization, and the like, we should expect the largest metropolitan areas—the areas where these symptoms of the modern era have furthest progressed—to have the highest crime rates with the rates decreasing as the population decreases. Table 1, compiled from the FBI's *Uniform Crime Reports* for 1974 (Table 5: "Index of Crime, 1974, Standard Metropolitan Statistical Areas," *UCR-1974*, pp. 73-90), shows that no such relationship is to be found.

    Nor does any relationship emerge when cities are compared by population density (number of persons per unit of space) instead of just by population. The President's Crime Commission, reporting on robbery rates in 1965 in the 14 largest cities, shows wildly different rates and virtually no correlation between the size of a city's population or its density and the incidence of robbery. Chicago and Philadelphia are roughly equal in population density, 15,836 and 15,743 persons per square mile respectively, while both are over five times as dense as Houston with 2860 persons per square mile. Neverthe-

less, Chicago has roughly three times as many robberies per
100,000 people as Philadelphia and Houston have. The 1965
rate for the City of Brotherly Love was 140 per 100,000 persons
and for the old Murder Capital it was 135, while Chicago came
in at an astounding 421, the highest in the nation. Meanwhile
the rate for New York (population density 24,697 persons per
square mile!) was lower than all three, and Washington, D.C.,
with roughly one tenth the population (763,956) and half the
density (12,442 persons per square mile) of New York City,
had over three times as many robberies per capita. Fun City's
rate in 1965 was a mere 114 per 100,000, while our nation's
capital came in second only to Chicago at 359. The commission
goes on to report that "Los Angeles is 1st for rape and 4th for
aggravated assault but 20th for murder, with a murder rate
less than half that of St. Louis. Chicago has the highest rate
for robbery but a relatively low rate for burglary. New York is
5th in larcenies $50 and over, but 54th for larcenies under $50.
The risk of auto theft is about 50 percent greater in Boston than
anywhere else in the country, but in Boston the likelihood of
other kinds of theft is about average for cities over 250,000."
Challenge, p. 29.

13. *Challenge*, p. 56.
14. *Time*, June 30, 1975, p. 11.
15. The number of Americans aged 15 to 24 arrested in 1974 was
2,959,289. In 1960, it was 1,112,827. In the decade of the 1950s
the crime rate increased 60 percent, from a rate of 1162.4 per
100,000 in 1950 to a rate of 1875.8 in 1960. Yet during that
same period the number of Americans aged 15 to 24 increased
only 9 percent and, as a percentage of the total population,
actually decreased from 14.7 percent in 1950 to 13.6 percent
in 1960. It was in the decade of the 1960s that the real impact
of the postwar baby boom was felt. By 1970 the number of
Americans between the ages of 15 and 24 increased dramatically. In 1970, there were 42 percent more persons aged 15 to 24
than there were in 1960, an increase of over 10 million souls.
But in the decade between 1960 and 1970, the crime rate increased by 111 percent! And in that same period the number of
15- to 24-year-olds arrested increased by 250 percent, from
1,112,827 to 2,838,230. Figures are from the United States Census Bureau, *Current Population Report*: Series P25, Number
519 and 614; and from the *UCR* for the relevant years.
16. *The Washington Post*, August 4, 1975, p. A2.

17. Ibid., August 17, 1975, pp. A1, A4.
18. Jeffrie G. Murphy, "Marxism and Retribution," *Philosophy and Public Affairs*, 2, No. 3 (Spring 1973), p. 237.
19. Franklin Zimring, *Firearms and Violence in American Life* (Washington, D.C.: U.S. Government Printing Office, 1968), pp. 6-7. (Emphasis added.)
20. Address by the Honorable Edward H. Levi, attorney general of the United States, before the Law Enforcement Executives Conference, April 6, 1975.
21. *Challenge*, p. 239 and p. 4. (Emphasis added.)
22. *The Washington Post*, November 18, 1975, p. A2. In 1976, these figures were down slightly: about 9 out of every 100,000 Americans were murdered, 64 percent of the murders were by firearm, 49 percent by handgun. *UCR-1976*, pp. 7, 9.
23. Zimring, *Firearms and Violence in American Life*, Chapter 11.
24. United States Department of Health, Education and Welfare, Public Health Service, National Institute on Alcohol Abuse and Alcoholism, Special Action Office for Drug Abuse Prevention, *Social Cost of Drug Abuse* (Washington, D.C., 1974), pp. 20-21.
25. "The largest study ever made of drug abuse in this country shows that two widely available legal drugs—alcohol and the tranquilizer Valium—are responsible for the greatest amount of drug-related illness, the government reported yesterday." Stuart Auerbach, "2 Drugs Widely Abused," *The Washington Post*, July 9, 1976, p. A1. See also Jeffrey H. Reiman, "Prostitution, Addiction, and the Ideology of Liberalism," in *Contemporary Crises* 3 (1979).
26. *Social Cost of Drug Abuse*, p. 25.
27. *UCR-1974*, p. 178. In 1976, the figure was a little over $4 billion, covering about 85 percent of the population. *UCR-1976*, p. 159.
28. Troy Duster, *The Legislation of Morality: Law, Drugs, and Moral Judgment* (New York: The Free Press, 1970), pp. 3, 7, inter alia.
29. Cf. Philip C. Baridon, *Addiction, Crime, and Social Policy* (Lexington, Mass.: Lexington Books, 1976), pp. 4-5.
30. *Time*, June 30, 1975, p. 17. (Emphasis added.)
31. Kai T. Erikson, *Wayward Puritans* (New York: John Wiley, copyright © 1966), p. 4. Reprinted by permission of John Wiley & Sons, Inc.
32. Ibid. p. 11.
33. Ibid. pp. 13-15. (Emphasis added.)

2

A Crime by Any Other Name

*If one individual inflicts a bodily injury
upon another which leads to the death
of the person attacked we call it manslaughter; on the other hand, if the
attacker knows beforehand that the
blow will be fatal we call it murder.
Murder has also been committed if
society places hundreds of workers in
such a position that they inevitably
come to premature and unnatural ends.
Their death is as violent as if they had
been stabbed or shot.... Murder has been
committed if society knows perfectly
well that thousands of workers cannot
avoid being sacrificed so long as these
conditions are allowed to continue.
Murder of this sort is just as culpable
as the murder committed by an
individual.*

  Frederick Engels, *The Condition of the
  Working Class in England*

a. What's in a Name?

If it takes you an hour to read this chapter, by the time you
reach the last page, two of your fellow citizens will have been
murdered. *During that same time, 11 Americans will die
from diseases due to unhealthy conditions in the workplace!*

Although these work-related deaths could have been prevented, they are not called murders. Why not? Doesn't a
crime by any other name still cause misery and suffering?
What's in a name?

The fact is that the label "crime" is not used in America to
name all or the worst of the actions that cause misery and
suffering to Americans. It is primarily reserved for the
dangerous actions of the poor.

In the March 14, 1976, edition of the *Washington Star*, a
front-page article appeared with the headline: "Mine Is
Closed 26 Deaths Late." The article read in part:

> Why, the relatives [of the 26 dead miners] ask, did the mine
> ventilation fail and allow pockets of volatile methane gas to
> build up in a shaft 2,300 feet below the surface?
>
> Why wasn't the mine cleared as soon as supervisors spotted
> evidence of methane gas near where miners were driving huge
> machines into the 61-foot-high coal seam?...
>
> In Washington, Sen. Harrison Williams, D-N.J., said inves-
> tigators of the Senate Labor and Welfare Committee which he
> chairs have found that there have been 1,250 safety violations
> at the 13-year-old mine since 1970. Fifty-seven of those viola-
> tions were serious enough for federal inspectors to order the
> mine closed and 21 of those were in cases where federal inspec-
> tors felt there was imminent danger to the lives of the miners
> working there, he said....
>
> Federal inspectors said the most recent violations found at
> the mine were three found in the ventilation system on Mon-
> day—the day before 15 miners were killed.[1]

Next to the continuation of this story was another, headlined: "Mass Murder Claims Six in Pennsylvania."[2] It described the shooting death of a husband and wife, their three
children, and a friend in a Philadelphia suburb. This was
murder, maybe even mass murder. My only question is, why
wasn't the death of the miners?

Why do 26 dead miners amount to a "disaster," and 6 dead
suburbanites a "mass murder"? "Murder" suggests a murder*er*, while "disaster" suggests the work of impersonal
forces. But if over 1000 safety violations had been found in
the mine—three the day before the first explosion—was no

one responsible for failing to eliminate the hazards? Was no one responsible for *preventing* the hazards? And if someone could have prevented the hazards and did not, does that person not bear responsibility for the deaths of 26 men? Is he less evil because he did not want them to die although he chose to leave them in jeopardy? Is he not a murderer, perhaps even a *mass* murderer?

These questions are at this point rhetorical. All the facts about the mine explosion at Oven Fork in the Kentucky mountains have not yet been studied. My aim is not to discuss this case but rather to point to the blinders we wear when we look at such a "disaster." Perhaps there will be an investigation. Perhaps someone will be held responsible. Perhaps he will be fined. But will he be tried for *murder?* Will anyone think of him as a murderer? *And if not, why not?* Would the miners not be safer if such people were treated as murderers? Might they not still be alive? Will the president of the United States address the Yale Law School and recommend mandatory prison sentences for such people? Will he mean these people when he says,

> These relatively few, persistent criminals who cause so much misery and fear are really the core of the problem. The rest of the American people have a right to protection from their violence [?][3]

Didn't those miners have a right to protection from the violence that took their lives? *And if not, why not?*

Once we are ready to ask this question seriously, we are in a position to see that the reality of crime—that is, the acts we label crime, the acts we think of as crime, the actors and actions we treat as criminal—is *created*: It is an image shaped by decisions as to *what* will be called crime and *who* will be treated as a criminal.

b. The Carnival Mirror

It is sometimes coyly observed that the quickest and cheapest way to eliminate crime would be to throw out all the criminal laws. There is a thin sliver of truth to this view. Without criminal laws, there would indeed be no "crimes." There would, however, still be dangerous acts. And this is why we cannot really solve our crime problem quite so simply. The criminal law *labels* some acts "crimes." In doing this, it identifies those acts as so dangerous that we must use the extreme methods of criminal justice to protect ourselves against them. But this does not mean that the criminal law *creates* crime—it simply "mirrors" real dangers that threaten us. And what is true of the criminal law is true of the whole justice system. If police did not arrest or prosecutors charge or juries convict, there would be no "criminals." But this does not mean that police or prosecutors or juries create criminals any more than legislators do. They *react* to real dangers in society. The criminal justice system—from lawmakers to law enforcers—is just a mirror of the real dangers that lurk in our midst. *Or so we are told.*

How accurate is this mirror? We need to answer this in order to know whether or how well the criminal justice system is protecting us against the real threats to our well-being. The more accurate a mirror, the more the image it shows is created by the reality it reflects. The more mis-shapen a mirror is, the more the distorted image it shows is created by the mirror, not by the reality reflected. It is in this sense that I will argue that the image of crime is created: The American criminal justice system is a mirror that shows a distorted image of the dangers that threaten us—an image created more by the shape of the mirror than by the reality reflected. What do we see when we look in the criminal justice mirror?

On the morning of September 16, 1975, the *Washington Post* carried an article in its local news section headlined "Arrest Data Reveals Profile of a Suspect." The article reported the results of a study of crime in Prince George's County, a suburb of Washington, D.C. It read in part,

> The typical suspect in serious crime in Prince George's County is a black male, aged 14 to 19, who lives in the area inside the Capital Beltway where more than half of the county's 64,371 reported crimes were committed in 1974....

[The study] presents a picture of persons, basically youths,
committing a crime once every eight minutes in Prince
George's County.[4]

This report is hardly a surprise. The portrait it paints of
"the typical suspect in serious crime" is probably a pretty
good rendering of the image lurking in the back of the minds
of most people who fear crime. Furthermore, although the
crime rate in Prince George's County is somewhat above the
national average and its black population somewhat above
that of the average suburban county, the portrait generally
fits the national picture presented in the FBI's *Uniform
Crime Reports* for the same year, 1974. In Prince George's
County, "Youths between the ages of 15 and 19 were accused
of committing nearly half [45.5 percent] of all 1974 crimes."[5]
For the nation, the FBI reports that persons in this age group
accounted for 39.5 percent of arrests for the FBI Index
Crimes (criminal homicide, forcible rape, robbery, aggravated assault, burglary, larceny, and motor vehicle theft.)[6]
In Prince George's County, where blacks make up approximately 25 percent of the population, "blacks were accused of
58 percent of all serious crimes."[7] In the nation, where blacks
make up 11.4 percent of the population, they account for 34.2
percent of the arrests for Index Crimes.[8] This is the Typical
Criminal. His is the face we see in the criminal justice mirror.
    He is, first of all, a *he*.[9] Second, he is a *youth*—most likely
under the age of 20. Third, he is predominantly *urban*—
although increasingly suburban.[10] Fourth, he is disproportionately *black*—blacks are arrested for Index Crimes at
a rate three times that of their percentage in the national population. And finally, he is *poor*: "Of the 1.3 million criminal
offenders handled each day by some agency of the United
States correctional system, the vast majority (80 percent on
some estimates) are members of the lowest 15-percent income
level—that percent which is below the 'poverty level' as defined by the Social Security Administration."[11] The President's Commission reports that "from arrest records, probation reports, and prison statistics, a 'portrait' of the offender
emerges that progressively highlights the disadvantaged

character of his life. The offender at the end of the road in prison is likely to be a member of the lowest social and economic groups in the country."[12]

This is the Typical Criminal feared by most law-abiding Americans. This is the Typical Criminal whose crime, according to former Attorney General John Mitchell (who is by no means a typical criminal), is forcing us "to change the fabric of our society," "forcing us, a free people to alter our pattern of life," "to withdraw from our neighbors, to fear all strangers and to limit our activities to 'safe' areas."[13] These poor, young, urban, (disproportionately) black males comprise the core of the enemy forces in the war against crime. They are the heart of a vicious unorganized guerrilla army, threatening the lives, limbs, and possessions of the law-abiding members of society—necessitating recourse to the ultimate weapons of force and detention in our common defense. They are the group President Ford had in mind when he spoke at Yale Law School, recommending mandatory prison sentences for convicted felons:

> Those who prey on others, especially by violence, are very, very few in number. A very small percentage of the whole population accounts for a very large proportion of the vicious crimes committed....[14]

And how do we know who the criminals are who so seriously endanger us that we must stop them with force and lock them in prisons?

"From arrest records, probation reports, and prison statistics," the authors of *The Challenge of Crime in a Free Society* tell us, the "'portrait' of the offender emerges."[15] *But these sources are not merely objective readings taken at different stages in the criminal justice process: each of them represents human decisions.* "Prison statistics" and "probation reports" reflect *decisions* of juries on who gets convicted, and decisions of judges on who gets probation or prison and for how long. "Arrest records" reflect *decisions* about which crimes to investigate and which suspects to take into custody. And all of these rest on the most fundamental of all *de-*

cisions: the decisions of legislators as to which acts shall be labeled "crimes" in the first place.

The reality of crime as the target of our criminal justice system and as perceived by the general populace is not a simple objective threat to which the system reacts: *it is a reality that takes shape as it is filtered through a series of human decisions running the full gamut of the criminal justice system*—from the lawmakers who determine what behavior shall be in the province of criminal justice to the law enforcers who decide which individuals will be brought within that province.

Our poor, young, urban, black male, who is so well represented in arrest records and prison populations, appears not simply because of the undeniable threat he poses to the rest of society. As dangerous as he may be, he would not appear in the criminal justice mirror *if* it had not been decided that the acts he performs should be labeled "crimes," *if* it had not been decided that he should be arrested for those crimes, *if* he had access to a lawyer who could persuade a jury to acquit him and perhaps a judge to expunge his arrest record, and *if* it had not been decided that he is the type of individual and his the type of crime that warrants imprisonment. *The shape of the reality we see in the criminal justice mirror is created by all these decisions.*

It is not my view that this reality is created out of nothing. The mugger, the rapist, the murderer, the burglar, the robber all pose a definite threat to our well-being, and they ought to be dealt with in ways that effectively reduce that threat to the minimum level possible, without making the criminal justice system itself a threat to our lives and liberties.

What is of central importance, however, is that the threat posed by the Typical Criminal is not the greatest threat to which we are exposed. The acts of the Typical Criminal are not the only acts that endanger us, nor are they the acts that endanger us the most. We have a greater chance *by far* (as I shall show below) of being killed or disabled by an occupational injury or disease, by unnecessary surgery, by shoddy emergency medical services, and much else, than by aggra-

vated assault or even homicide! Yet even though these
threats to our well-being are far graver than that posed by
our poor, young, urban, black males, they do not show up in
the FBI's Index of serious crimes! And the individuals who
are responsible for them do not turn up in arrest records or
prison statistics. *They never become part of the reality reflected in the criminal justice mirror, although the danger they
pose is at least as great and often greater than those who do!*

Similarly the general public loses more money *by far* (as I
shall show below) from price-fixing and monopolistic practices, and from consumer deception and embezzlement, than
from all the property crimes in the FBI's Index combined. Yet
these far more costly acts are either not criminal, or if technically criminal, not prosecuted, or if prosecuted, not punished,
or if punished, only mildly. In any event, although the individuals responsible for these acts take more money out of the
ordinary citizen's pocket than our Typical Criminal, they
rarely show up in arrest statistics and almost never in prison
populations. *Their faces rarely appear in the criminal justice
mirror, although the danger they pose is at least as great and
often greater than those who do.*

The inescapable conclusion is that the criminal justice system does not simply *reflect* the reality of crime; it has a hand
in *creating* the reality we see.

The criminal justice system is like a mirror in which
society can see the face of the evil in its midst. But because
the system deals with some evil and not with others, because
it treats some evils as the gravest and treats some of the gravest evils as minor, the image it throws back is distorted like
the image in a *carnival mirror*. And like a carnival mirror,
the image cast back is false, not because it is invented out of
thin air, but because the proportions of the real are distorted:
large becomes small and small large, grave becomes minor
and minor grave. And like a carnival mirror, although nothing is reflected that does not exist in the world, the image
is more a creation of the mirror than a picture of the world.

If criminal justice really gives us a carnival-mirror image
of "crime," we are doubly deceived. First, we are led to believe

that the criminal justice system is protecting us against the
gravest threats to our well-being when, in fact, the system is
only protecting us against some threats and not necessarily
the gravest ones. The second deception is less obvious and
more vicious. It flows from the fact that people believe the
first one. If people believe that the carnival mirror is a true
mirror—that is, if they believe that the criminal justice system simply *reacts* to the gravest threats to their well-being—
they come to believe that whatever is the target of the criminal justice system must be the greatest threat to their well-
being. In other words, if people believe that the most drastic
of society's weapons are wielded by the criminal justice system *in reaction to* the gravest dangers to society, they will
come to believe the reverse as well: that those actions that
call forth the most drastic of society's weapons *must be* those
that pose the gravest dangers to society.

There is a strange alchemy that takes place when people
uncritically accept the legitimacy of their institutions: what
needs justification becomes *proof* of justification. People
come to believe that prisoners must be criminals *because*
they are in prison and that the inmates of insane asylums
must be crazy *because* they are in insane asylums.[16] The use
of extreme measures—such as force and imprisonment—by
the criminal justice system is thought to be justified by the
extreme gravity of the dangers it combats. But by this alchemy, these extreme measures become *proof* of the extreme
gravity of those dangers, and the first deception—which
merely misleads the public about how much protection the
criminal justice system is actually providing—is transformed into the second—which deceives the public into be-
lieving that the acts and actors that are the target of the
criminal justice system pose the gravest threats to its well-
being. Thus the system may not only fail to protect us from
dangers as great or greater than those listed in the FBI
Crime Index, but it may do still greater damage by creating
the false security of the belief that only the acts on the FBI
Index really threaten us and require control.

In the following discussion, I will try to describe how and

1.)   why the criminal justice carnival mirror distorts the image it
      creates.

c. Criminal Justice as Creative Art

In Chapter 1, I introduced the Pyrrhic defeat explanation for
the "failure" of criminal justice in America: criminal justice
fails (or, what amounts to the same thing, crime is maintained) in order to project a particular *image* of crime.

   It is the task of this chapter and the next to prove that the
reality of crime—that is, the acts we label "crime," the acts
we think of as crime, the actors and actions we treat as
criminal— is *created* and that it is created in a way that promotes a particular *image* of crime: *The image that serious
crime—and therefore the greatest danger to society—is the
work of the poor*. The notion that the reality of crime is
created is derived from Richard Quinney's theory of *the social reality of crime*.[17] Since the meaning I attribute to this
notion is somewhat different from the meaning Quinney
gives it, it will help in presenting my view to compare it to
Quinney's.

   Quinney maintains that crime has a "social reality" rather
than an objective reality. What he means can be explained
with an example. Wherein lies the reality of money? Certainly not in the "objective" characteristics of green printed
paper. It exists rather in the "social" meaning attributed to
that paper and the pattern of "social" behavior that is a consequence of that meaning. If people did not act as if that
green printed paper had value, it would be just green paper,
not real money. The reality of a crime *as a crime* does not
lie simply in the objective characteristics of an action. It lies
in the "social" meaning attached to that action and the pattern of "social" behavior—particularly the behavior of criminal justice officials—which is a product of that meaning. I
think Quinney is right in this. When I speak of the reality of
crime, I am referring to much more than physical actions like
stabbing or shooting. I am referring to the reality that a

society gives those physical actions by labeling them criminal and treating them as criminal.

Quinney further maintains that this reality of crime is *created*. By this he means that crime is a definition of behavior applied by lawmakers and other criminal justice decision makers. "Crime," Quinney writes, "is a *definition* of behavior that is conferred on some persons by others. Agents of the law (legislators, police, prosecutors, and judges), representing segments of a politically organized society, are responsible for formulating and administering criminal laws. Persons and behaviors, therefore, become criminal because of the *formulation* and *application* of criminal definitions. Thus, *crime is created*."[18]

Now this is *not* what I have in mind when I say that the reality of crime is created. Here is the difference. Quinney's position amounts to this: crimes are established by the criminal law and the criminal law is a human creation; ergo, crime is created. This is true, but it does not take us very far. After all, who can deny that crime is created *in this sense*? Only someone who has been hypnotized into forgetting that law books are written by lawmakers could deny that "crime" is a label that human beings apply to certain actions. What *is* controversial, however, is whether or not the label is applied appropriately. "Crime" after all is not merely a sound—it is a word with a generally accepted meaning. It means roughly "an intentional action that is harmful to society." The label is applied appropriately when it is used to identify all, or at least the worst of, the acts that are harmful to society. The label is applied inappropriately when it is attached to any harmless act *or* when it is not attached to seriously harmful acts. When I argue that the reality of crime is created, what I mean is that the label "crime" has not been applied appropriately.

One might ask why the inappropriate use of the label "crime" is a reason for saying that crime is created. My answer is this: By calling something *created*, we call attention to the fact that human actors are responsible for it. By calling crime created, I mean to call attention to the fact that human actors—particularly criminal justice decision makers—are responsible for the shape it takes. Now if the label "crime" is applied appropriately, this means that its content is dictated by objective facts—real harm, independent of our decisions. If the label "crime" is consistently applied to the most harmful acts, then it is misleading to point to the fact that decision makers are responsible for it, since their decisions are dictated by compelling objective reasons. On the other hand, if the label is not applied appropriately, then it can no longer be said that those who apply the label are compelled by objective reasons. In that event, it is sensible to assume that the label is applied for reasons that lie with the decision makers and not out in the realm of objective fact. This means that when the label "crime" is applied inappropriately, it is of utmost importance to call attention to the fact that human actors—particularly criminal justice decision makers—are responsible for it. In other words, it is precisely when the label "crime" is applied inappropriately that it is important to point out that the reality of crime is *created*.

By calling crime created, I want to emphasize the human responsibility for the shape of crime, not in the trivial sense that humans write the criminal law, *but rather to call attention to the fact that decisions as to what to label and treat as crime are not compelled by objective dangers and thus that to understand the reality of crime, we must look to the motives and interests of those who shape those decisions.*

By calling crime created, I want to point to the fact that our picture of crime—the portrait that emerges from arrest statistics, prison populations, politicians' speeches, news media, and fictionalized presentations, the portrait that in turn influences lawmakers and criminal justice policymakers—is not a photograph of the real dangers that threaten us. Its features are not simply traced from the real dangers in the social world. Instead, it is a piece of creative art. It is a picture in which some dangers are portrayed and others omitted. And since it cannot be explained as a straight reflection of real dangers, we must look elsewhere to understand the shape it takes.

This argument, which will occupy us in this chapter and

the next, can be viewed as an attempt to establish the truth of *five hypotheses* about the way in which criminal justice policy is made. To demonstrate that the reality of crime is created, that the criminal justice system is a carnival mirror that gives us a distorted image of the dangers that threaten us, I will try to prove that at each of the crucial decision-making points in criminal justice, the decisions made do not reflect the real and most serious dangers we face.

Of the Decisions of Legislators
1. That the definitions of crime in the criminal law do not reflect the only or the most dangerous of antisocial behaviors.

Of the Decisions of Police and Prosecutors
2. That the decisions on whom to arrest or charge do not reflect the only or the most dangerous behaviors legally defined as "criminal."

Of the Decisions of Juries and Judges
3. That criminal convictions do not reflect the only or the most dangerous individuals among those arrested and charged.

Of the Decisions of Sentencing Judges
4. That sentencing decisions do not reflect the goal of protecting society from the only or the most dangerous of those convicted by meting out punishments proportionate to the harmfulness of the crime committed.

And of All These Decisions Taken Together
5. That what criminal justice policy decisions (in hypotheses 1 to 4) *do* reflect is the implicit identification of crime with the dangerous acts of the poor.

The Pyrrhic defeat theory is composed of these five propositions, *plus* the proposition that the criminal justice system is failing in avoidable ways to reduce crime (argued in Chapter 1) *and* the proposition that failure in this form serves the interests of the powerful by conveying an ideological message (argued in Chapter 4).

d.   A Crime by Any Other Name...

Think of a crime, any crime. Picture the first "crime" that comes into your mind. What do you see? The odds are you are not imagining a mining company executive sitting at his desk, calculating the costs of proper safety precautions and deciding not to invest in them. The odds are that what you do see with your mind's eye is one person physically attacking another or robbing something from another on the threat of physical attack. Look more closely. What does the attacker look like? It's a safe bet he (and it is a *he*, of course) is not wearing a suit and tie. In fact, my hunch is that you—like me, like almost anyone in America—picture a young, tough, lower-class male when the thought of crime first pops into your head. You (we) picture someone like the Typical Criminal described above. And the crime itself is one in which our Typical Criminal sets out to attack or rob some specific person.

This last point is important. What it indicates is that we have a mental image not only of the Typical Criminal, but also of the Typical Crime. If the Typical Criminal is a young lower-class male, the Typical Crime is *one-on-one harm*— where harm means either physical injury or loss of something valuable or both. If you have any doubts that this is the Typical Crime, look at any random sample of police or private eye shows on television. How often do you see Jim Rockford investigate consumer fraud or failure to remove occupational hazards? In fact, since portraying young lower-class males becomes rather humdrum after a steady diet, while one-on-one harm is apparently inexhaustibly interesting, the networks are much more likely to diverge from the Typical Criminal than from the Typical Crime. So even when a TV show such as "Columbo" specializes in crimes by the well-to-do in the California "Castle Circuit," the crimes they commit are basically the same as those that occupy Kojak on grubby New York sidestreets: crimes of one-on-one harm.

It is important to identify this model of the Typical Crime because it functions like a set of blinders. It keeps us from calling a mine disaster a mass murder even if 26 men are killed, even if someone is responsible for the unsafe conditions in which they worked and died. In fact, I will argue that this particular piece of mental furniture so blocks our view that it keeps us from using the criminal justice system to protect ourselves from the greatest threats to our persons and possessions!

What keeps a mine disaster from being a mass murder in our eyes is the fact that it is not a one-on-one harm. What is important here is not the numbers but the *specificity of intent to do harm*. An attack by a gang on one or more persons or an attack by one individual on several fits the model of one-on-one harm. What is important is that for each person harmed there is at least one individual who wanted to harm that person specifically. Once he selects his victim, the rapist, the mugger, the murderer, all want *this* person they have selected to suffer. Our mine executive on the other hand does not want his employees to be harmed. He would truly prefer that there be no accident, no injured or dead miners. What he does want is something legitimate. It is what he has been hired to get: maximum profits at minimum costs. If he cuts corners to save a buck, he is just doing his job. If 26 men die because he cut corners on safety, we may think him crude or callous but not a killer. He is, at most, responsible for an *indirect harm*, not a one-on-one harm. For this, he may even be criminally indictable for violating safety regulations— but not for murder. The 26 men are dead as an unwanted consequence of his (perhaps overzealous or undercautious) pursuit of a legitimate goal. And so, unlike the Typical Criminal, he has not committed the Typical Crime. Or so we generally believe. As a result, 26 men are dead who might be alive now if the kind of corner-cutting that leads to loss of life, whether suffering is specifically intended or not, were treated as murder.

This is my point. Because we accept the belief—encouraged by our politicians' statements about crime and by the media's portrayal of crime—that the model for crime is one person specifically intending to harm another, we accept a legal system that leaves us unprotected against much greater dangers to our lives and well-being than those threatened by the Typical Criminal. Before developing this point further, let us anticipate and deal with a likely objection. The defender of the present legal order is likely to respond to my argument at this point with irritation. Since this will surely turn to outrage in a few pages, let us talk to him now while the possibility of rational communication still exists.

The Defender of the Present Legal Order (I'll call him "the Defender" for short whenever it is necessary to deal with his objections in the future) is neither a foolish nor an evil person. He is not a racist, nor is he oblivious to the need for reform in the criminal justice system to make it more even-handed and for reform in the larger society to make equal opportunity a reality for all Americans. In general, his view is that—given our limited resources, particularly the resource of human altruism—the political and legal institutions we have are the best that can be. What is necessary is to make them work better and to weed out those who are intent on making them work shoddily. His response to my argument at this point is that the criminal justice system *should* occupy itself primarily with one-on-one harm. Harms of the sort exemplified in the "mine disaster" are really *not* murders and are better dealt with through stricter government enforcement of safety regulations. He would admit that this enforcement has been rather lax and recommend that it be improved. But basically he thinks this division of labor is right because it fits our ordinary moral sensibilities. In other words, according to our ordinary moral notions, someone who wants to do another harm and does is really more evil than someone who jeopardizes others while pursuing legitimate goals but wishes no one harm. And thus the former is rightfully in the province of the criminal justice system with its drastic weapons, while the latter is appropriately dealt with by milder forms of regulation.

I think the Defender's argument rests on two errors. First, it treats our ordinary notions of morality as a single consistent fabric rather than the crazy quilt of conflicting values and ideals it is. In other words, even if it fits some of our ordinary moral notions to believe that one-on-one harm is more evil than indirect harm, other aspects of our ordinary moral sensibilities lead to the opposite conclusion. For instance, compare our corner-cutting mine executive to the typical murderer. Most murders, we know, are committed in the heat of some garden-variety passion like rage or jealousy. Two lovers or neighbors or relatives find themselves in a heated argument. One (usually it is a matter of chance *which* one) picks up a weapon and strikes the other a fatal blow. Such a person is clearly a murderer and rightly subject to treatment by the criminal justice system. I make no bones about this. But is this person more evil than our executive who chooses not to pay for safety equipment? I think a perfectly good case can be made that starts with our ordinary moral notions and ends up with the opposite conclusion.

The one who kills in a heated argument kills from passion. What he does he probably would not do in a cooler moment. He is likely to feel "he was not himself." The one he killed was someone he knew, a specific someone who at the time seemed to him to be the embodiment of all that frustrates him, someone whose very existence makes life unbearable. I do not mean to suggest that this is true of all killers, although there is reason to believe it is true of many. Nor do I mean to suggest that such a state of mind justifies murder. What it does do, however, is suggest that the passion killer's action does not show general disdain for the lives of his fellows. Here is where he is different from the doer of *indirect harm*. Our absentee killer intended harm to no one in particular, but he *knew his acts were likely to harm someone*—and once someone is harmed, *he* (the victim) is someone in particular. Nor can our absentee killer claim that "he was not himself." His act is done, not out of passion, but out of cool reckoning. And precisely here his evil shows. In his willingness to jeopardize the lives of unspecified others who pose him no real or imaginary threat in order to make a few dollars, he shows his general disdain for all his fellow human beings. In this light, it is surely absurd to hold that he is less evil than the passion killer. My point will be made if you merely agree that both are equally wicked.

The Defender's argument errs a second time by overlooking the role of legal institutions in shaping our ordinary moral notions. Many who defend the criminal justice system do so precisely because of its function in educating the public about the difference between right and wrong. The great historian of English law, Sir James Fitzjames Stephens, held that a "great part of the general detestation of crime which happily prevails amongst the decent part of the community in all civilized countries arises from the fact that the commission of offences is associated in all such communities with the solemn and deliberate infliction of punishment wherever crime is proved."[19] In other words, one cannot simply appeal to ordinary moral notions to defend the criminal law, since the criminal law has already had a hand in shaping ordinary moral notions. At least one observer has argued that making narcotics use a crime in the beginning of this century *caused* a change in the public's ordinary moral notions about drug addiction, which prior to that time had been viewed as a medical problem.[20] It is probably safe to say that in our own time, civil rights legislation has sharpened the public's moral condemnation of racial discrimination. Hence we might speculate that if the criminal justice system began to prosecute—and if the media began to portray— those who inflict *indirect harm* as serious criminals, our ordinary moral notions would change on this point as well.

I think this disposes of the Defender for the time being, although we shall surely hear from him again. We are left with the conclusion that there is no moral basis for treating *indirect harm* as less evil than *one-on-one harm*. What matters, then, is whether the purpose of the criminal justice system will be served by including, in the category of serious crime, harm caused without the intention to harm a specific individual.

What is the purpose of the criminal justice system? No eso-
teric answer is required. Norval Morris and Gordon Hawkins
write that "the prime function of the criminal law is to protect our persons and our property."[21] *The Challenge of Crime
in a Free Society*, the report of the President's Commission
on Law Enforcement and Administration of Justice, tells us
that "any criminal justice system is an apparatus society
uses to enforce the standards of conduct necessary to protect
individuals and the community."[22] Whatever else we think a
criminal justice system should accomplish, I doubt if anyone
would deny that its central purpose is to protect us against
the most serious threats to our well-being. I will argue that
this purpose is seriously undermined by taking one-on-one
harm as the model of crime. Excluding harm caused without
the intention to harm a specific individual prevents the
criminal justice system from protecting our persons and our
property from dangers at least as great as those posed by one-
on-one harm. This is so because, as I will show, there are a
large number of actions that are not labeled *criminal* but that
lead to loss of life, limb, and possessions on a scale comparable to those actions that are represented in the FBI
Crime Index. And a crime by any other name still causes
misery and suffering.

* * *

In the remainder of this section I will identify some acts
that are *crimes by any other name*—that is, acts that cause
harm and suffering comparable to that caused by acts that
are called crimes. My purpose is to confirm the first hypothesis: that the definitions of crime in the criminal law do not
reflect the only or the most dangerous antisocial behaviors.
To do this, we will need some measure of the harm and suffering caused by crimes with which we can compare the harm
and suffering caused by noncrimes. Our measure need not be
too refined, since my point can be made if I can show that
there are some acts that we do not treat as crime but that
cause harm *roughly comparable* to that caused by crimes. It
will be satisfactory for these purposes, then, to construct a

rough measure from the findings in the *FBI Uniform Crime Reports*, which covers crime for 1974.

According to the *UCR*, 1974 saw 20,600 murders and non-negligent manslaughters. During that year, there were 452,720 reported cases of aggravated assault, 55,210 reported instances of forcible rape, and 441,290 reported robberies. These are the offenses that the *UCR* includes in the class of violent crimes. "Murder and nonnegligent manslaughter" includes "all willful felonious homicides as distinguished from deaths caused by negligence." "Forcible rape" refers to "the carnal knowledge of a female, forcibly and against her will in the categories of rape by force, assault to rape and attempted rape," with the exception of statutory rape (no force used, but the victim is under age of consent). "Aggravated assault" is defined as "assault with intent to kill or for the purpose of inflicting severe bodily injury by shooting, cutting, stabbing, maiming, poisoning, scalding, or by the use of acids, explosives, or other means." Finally the category of "robbery" includes "stealing or taking anything of value from the care, custody, or control of a person by force or by violence or by putting in fear, such as strong-arm robbery, stickups, armed robbery, assaults to rob, and attempts to rob."[23] Now, since robbery is generally done on threat of injury rather than actual injury, the number of robberies is not a direct indicator of physical harm, while the number of aggravated assaults and forcible rapes is. Thus, as a measure of the physical harm done by crime in 1974, I shall assume that reported crimes led to roughly 20,000 deaths and half a million instances of serious bodily harm short of death.

We need a measure of loss of property as well. The *UCR* reports the total value of property stolen in 1974 as $2,616,600,000. Since this is based on reports from criminal justice agencies serving somewhat more than three-fourths of the nation's population, it is undoubtedly low as a national total, even allowing that individuals reporting thefts may inflate the value of the stolen property for a number of reasons. Let us say, then, that the value of property lost to thieves (including stolen currency) during 1974 is somewhere between 3 and 3½ billion dollars.[24]

These, then, are the figures I will use. Any actions that lead to loss of even a sizable fraction of the 20,000 lives taken by murder and nonnegligent manslaughter, any actions that do serious physical harm to even a sizable fraction of the half million persons victimized by aggravated assault and forcible rape, any actions that lead to unjustifiable loss of even a sizable fraction of the 3 to 3½ billion dollars lost to thieves are clearly grave dangers to the community. They are surely precisely the kind of harmful actions from which a criminal justice system whose purpose is to protect our persons and property ought to protect us. *They are crimes by other names.*

Once we use these figures, it is hard to avoid the conclusion that the most dangerous American crime ring since the days of Al Capone is the United States government. The Vietnam War, based on a history of deception predating even the lies we were told about the so-called Gulf of Tonkin incident,[25] stands without peer in recent years in the annals of unnecessary carnage wrought by American hands. Few observers of Vietnamese history doubt that the present condition—more or less peaceful consolidation of South and North Vietnam under a more or less independent Communist regime—could have been achieved by negotiations with Ho Chi Minh many years, many lives, and many dollars ago. Furthermore, we need not doubt that those who consistently lied to the American public—as the Pentagon Papers amply document— knew that the American people would not willingly send their sons and their treasure to defend a dictator like Nguyen Van Thieu against his own people. Thus, those who perpetrated this war have on their hands the blood of over 50,000 American boys who would be alive today if American military policy was limited to protecting America's real interests and not carried on behind a shroud of lies. In addition to more than 50,000 dead Americans, they are responsible for several hundred thousand wounded Americans, many permanently injured, not to say all the hundreds of thousands (some estimates go well over a million) of South Vietnamese who were killed by our troops and bombers as we fought to make their land safe for democracy!

I mention the Vietnam War, not because I believe that its perpetrators are likely to be brought to justice for the suffering they caused—or for the roughly $164 billion they took from the pockets of American taxpayers to finance their carnage—but because I wish to inject a note of humility which is often missing in discussions of our "crime problem." As indignant as we may be at the mugger or rapist or murderer, we should never forget that they are small change compared to our own leaders when it comes to causing needless suffering, and they are much more likely to suffer before and as a result of their acts than our leaders ever will.

Coming closer to home, the case that there are noncriminal actions that are more dangerous than the crimes on the FBI's Index can be made just by looking at occupational hazards in America.

1. *Work May Be Dangerous to Your Health*

Since the publication of *The President's Report on Occupational Safety and Health*[26] in 1972, numerous studies have documented both the astounding incidence of disease, injury, and death due to hazards in the workplace *and* the fact that much or most of this carnage is the avoidable consequence of the refusal of management to pay for safety measures and of government to enforce safety standards.[27]

In that 1972 report, the government sets the number of job-related illnesses at 390,000 per year and the number of annual deaths from industrial disease at 100,000.[28] Just as raw numbers, these findings suggest that holding a job in America is about five times as deadly as murder and nonnegligent manslaughter and nearly as likely to harm you nonlethally as aggravated assault. But the actual tale told by these figures is much worse when the following factors are taken into consideration.

- Our measure of harm from crime is based on 1974 figures. To be strictly comparable with the figures on industrial death and disease, we should cite 1972 crime statistics. The relevant figures are 18,570 murders and nonnegligent manslaughters in 1972 and 436,770 aggravated assaults and forcible rapes during that same year.[29]
- The risk of job-related death or disease falls only on members of the labor force, while the risk of crime falls on the whole population, from infants to old folks. Since the labor force is less than half the total population, to get a true picture of the relative threat posed by occupational diseases compared to that posed by crime we should *halve* the crime statistics when comparing them to the figures for industrial disease and death. Using statistics for 1972, this means the *comparable* figures would be:

	Occupational Hazard	*Crime*
Death	100,000	9,285
Other physical harm	390,000	218,385

If it is argued that this paints an inaccurate picture because so many crimes go unreported, my answer is this. First of all, homicides are by far the most completely reported of crimes. For obvious reasons, the general underreporting of crimes is not equal among crimes. It is much easier or tempting to avoid reporting a rape or a mugging than a corpse. Second, aggravated assaults, which make up about 90 percent of the figure I have been using for nonfatal crime-produced injury, are among the better-reported crimes, although not the best. On the other hand, since occupational diseases and deaths are likely to cost firms money in the form of workdays lost and insurance premiums raised, since occupational diseases are frequently first seen by company physicians who have every reason to diagnose complaints as either non-job-related or malingering, and since many occupationally caused diseases do not show symptoms or lead to death until after the employee has left the job, we should expect *more*—not less—underreporting of industrial than criminal victims. In fact,

> A survey conducted last year by the University of Washington reported that one in four Americans currently suffers an occupational disease. The report also disclosed that only one of the 10 workers with an occupational disease had been included in either OSHA [Occupational Safety and Health Administration] statistics or in the state's workmen's compensation records.[30]

It should be further noted that the statistics given so far are for occupational *diseases* and deaths from those diseases. They do not include death and injury from industrial *accidents*. Here, too, the statistics are gruesome:

> The National Safety Council reported that in 1970 industrial accidents caused 14,200 deaths and 2.2 million disabling work injuries; 245 million man-days lost because of work accidents; $1.8 billion in wage losses; $900 million in medical costs; and a total cost to the economy in the amount of over $9 billion.[31]

This brings the total number of occupation-related deaths to over 114,000 a year.

The magnitude of the human cost of American "prosperity"—the quantity of blood and pain that goes into the endless bounty of consumer goods that line store shelves—is hard to grasp. One writer, trying to translate the figures into terms with which we are familiar, asks,

> Have you ever seen a notice in the news that after the predictable 300-to-400 die in traffic this weekend, more than 2000 will perish next week "just from trying to make a living"?[32]

Can there be any doubt that workers are more likely to stay alive and healthy in the face of anything the underworld can dish out than in the face of what their employers have in store for them on the job? If any doubt lingers, consider this. Lest we falter in the struggle against crime, the FBI includes

in their annual *Uniform Crime Reports* a table of "crime
clocks," which graphically illustrates the extent of the criminal menace. For 1974, the crime clock shows a murder occur-
ring every 26 minutes.[33] If a similar crime clock for industrial
deaths were constructed—still using the 1970 and 1972 figures cited above and recalling that this clock ticks only for
that half of the population that is in the labor force—this
clock would show an industrial death about every 4½ minutes! In other words, in the time it takes for one murder on the
crime clock, six workers have died "just from trying to make
a living"!

To say that some of these workers died from accidents due
to their own carelessness is about as helpful as saying that
some of those who died at the hands of murderers asked for it.
It overlooks the fact that where workers are careless, it is not
because they love to live dangerously. They have production
quotas to meet, quotas that they themselves do not set. If
quotas were set with an eye to keeping work at a safe pace
rather than to keeping the production-to-wages ratio as high
as possible, it might be more reasonable to expect workers to
take the time to be careful. Beyond this, we should bear in
mind that the vast majority of occupational deaths result
from disease, not accident, and disease is generally a function of conditions outside a worker's control, such as the level
of coal dust in the air (about 10 percent of all active coal
miners have black lung disease),[34] or textile dust (more than
"seventeen thousand active cotton, flax, and hemp workers
suffer from byssinosis, or brown lung"),[35] or asbestos fibers
(a study of 632 asbestos-insulation workers between 1943
and 1971 indicates that 11 percent have died of asbestosis
and 38 percent of cancer; two doctors who have studied
asbestos workers conclude "we can anticipate three thousand excess respiratory, cardiopulmonary deaths and cancers of the lung—three thousand excess deaths *annually* for
the next twenty or thirty years"),[36] or coal tars ("workers who
had been employed five or more years in the coke ovens died
of lung cancer at a rate three and a half times that for all
steelworkers"; coke oven workers also develop cancer of the

scrotum at a rate five times that of the general population).[37] Blaming it on the workers also does not account for the fact that some 800,000 people suffer from occupationally related skin disease each year (according to a 1968 estimate by the U.S. surgeon general)[38] or that "the number of American workers experiencing noise conditions that may damage their hearing is estimated [in a 1969 Public Health Service publication of the Department of Health, Education and Welfare] to be in excess of 6 million, and may even reach 16 million."[39]

But most importantly, blaming it on the workers simply ignores the history of governmental attempts to compel industrial firms to meet safety standards that would keep dangers (such as chemicals or fibers or dust particles in the air) that are outside of the worker's control down to a safe minimum. This has been a continual struggle, with firms using everything from their own "independent" research institutes to more direct and often questionable forms of political pressure, to influence government in the direction of loose standards and lax enforcement. So far, industry has been winning: Nearly 600,000 workers have been killed on the job since President Nixon signed into law the bill creating the Occupational Safety and Health Administration, a bill "designed to put an end to injury and death in the American workplace."[40]

The reason for this is that OSHA has been given neither the personnel nor the mandate to make good on this promise. It is so understaffed that "in 1973, when 1500 Federal sky marshalls guarded the nation's airplanes from hijackers, only 500 OSHA inspectors toured the nation's [5 million] workplaces." OSHA's budget is also an indication of the low priority given occupational health and safety: "The Federal government this year [1976] has budgeted $116 million for the Occupational Safety and Health Administration compared with $148 million to support commissaries on U.S. military bases." The Office of Management and Budget cut the fiscal 1976 budget request for $43 million for researching job-related health hazards to $32 million: "The bulk of the cuts

involved research programs on occupationally caused cancers."[41] In addition to this, although OSHA has the power to
levy fines for safety violations, its major thrust is on *voluntary compliance*, but since the chance of inspection is low
and since fines are low when they are levied, there is little
reason for firms to comply voluntarily, and so there is little
voluntary compliance.

> During fiscal 1972, OSHA was able to make only about 33,000
> inspections at workplaces employing a total of 6 million
> workers. It is estimated that with its currently available re-
> sources, OSHA can inspect every workplace covered by the act
> only once in every 40 years.
>
>   With so few inspections possible, only by applying strict
> penalties to violators could OSHA have a chance of enforcing
> the law. During fiscal 1972, inspectors found violations in 75%
> of the workplaces inspected, and fined 45% of the employers.
> The average fine for a violation was $22.60, and $99.00 was the
> average total per workplace. It is clear that such fines could
> provide no incentive for even small businesses to clean up, let
> alone giants like General Motors or Standard Oil. Thus the
> most profitable plan for an employer is to violate the law, hope
> that no inspection takes place, pay the fine if an inspection
> does take place, and perhaps do a little cleaning up in response
> to the inspection.[42]

Bitter Wages, the Nader Group's report, recounts a similar
tale at the level of state enforcement of safety standards. In
25 states sampled in 1968 by the AFL-CIO, "one and a half
times as many game wardens as safety inspectors" were employed.[43] The Nader Group sums up the situation at the state
level in these terms:

> The real weakness in the administration of state safety codes
> stems from the philosophical approach to enforcement taken
> by virtually all the states. The strange notion has become
> deeply rooted that corporate lawbreakers should not be penal-
> ized, but merely warned, in order to give them the opportunity
> for "voluntary compliance" with safety regulations.... *The
> record indicates that this hope remains unfulfilled.* Employers

have little incentive to take any initiative to root out unsafe
work conditions and practices. Instead, they can subject their
employees to all kinds of hazards, to be corrected only if discovered by state inspectors—if and when the plant is visited.[44]

Over and over again, the same story appears. Workers
begin to sicken and die at a plant. They call on their employer to lower the level of hazardous material in the air, and
their employer responds first by denying that a hazard
exists. As the corpses pile up, the firm's scientists "discover"
that some danger does exist but that it can be removed by reducing the hazardous material to a "safe" level—which is
still above what independent and government researchers
think is really safe. At this point, government and industry
spar about "safe" levels and usually compromise at a level in
between—something less dangerous than industry wants
but still dangerous. This does not mean that the new levels
are met, even if written into the law. So government inspectors and compliance officers must come in, and when (and if)
they do, their efforts are too little and too late:

• Federal officials cited the Beryllium Corporation for 26
  safety violations and 5 "serious violations" for "excessive
  beryllium concentration in work place areas." Fine: $928.
  The corporation's net sales for 1970 were $61,400,000.[45]
• On request from the Oil, Chemical and Atomic Workers
  Union, OSHA officials inspected the Mobil Oil plant at
  Paulsboro, New Jersey. Result: citations for 354 violations of the Occupational Health and Safety Act of 1970.
  Fine: $7350 (about $20 a violation).[46]
• In 1972, a fire and explosion at the same Mobil plant
  killed a worker. Fine: $1215.[47]
• In 1968, there were 24,845 safety violations in Massachu-
  setts, 28 prosecutions, 12 fines. Average fine: $88.[48]
• That same year, New York employers committed over
  10,000 safety violations. The State Division of Inspection
  and Safety referred 442 cases for prosecution. Result: six
  fines.[49]

- Adam Walinsky "released a confidential state labor department memo which revealed that of 1,228 deaths from
  industrial accidents in 1968, only 140 had been inves-
  tigated, and that in fifty-eight of the 140 instances, 'violations of the industrial code of the New York State Labor
  Law were identified as contributing to the accident.'
  There were no prosecutions."[50]

And so it goes on.

Is a person who kills another in a bar brawl a greater
threat to society than a business executive who refuses to cut
into his profits in order to make his plant a safe place to
work? By any measure of death and suffering the latter is by
far a greater danger than the former. But because he wishes
his workers no harm, because he is only indirectly responsible for death and disability while pursuing legitimate economic goals, his acts are not called *crimes*. Once we free our
imagination from the irrational shackle of the one-on-one
model of crime, can there be any doubt that the criminal justice system does *not* protect us from the gravest threats to
life and limb? It seeks to protect us when that threat comes
from a young, lower-class male in the inner city. When that
threat comes from an upper-class business executive in an
office, it looks the other way. And this in the face of growing
evidence that for every American citizen murdered by some
thug, six American workers are killed by their bosses.

2.   Health Care May Be Dangerous to Your Health

About ten years ago, when the annual number of willful homicides in the nation was about 10,000, the President's Commission on Law Enforcement and Administration of Justice
reported that

> A recent study of emergency medical care found the quality,
> numbers, and distribution of ambulances and other emergency
> services severely deficient, and estimated that as many as

20,000 Americans die unnecessarily each year as a result of improper emergency care. The means necessary for correcting this situation are very clear and would probably yield greater immediate return in reducing death than would expenditures for reducing the incidence of crimes of violence.[51]

On July 15, 1975, Dr. Sidney Wolfe of Ralph Nader's Public Interest Health Research Group testified before the House Commerce Oversight and Investigations Subcommittee that there "were 3.2 million cases of unnecessary surgery performed each year in the United States." These unneeded operations, Dr. Wolfe added, "cost close to $5 billion a year and kill as many as 16,000 Americans."[52] Wolfe's estimates of unnecessary surgery were based on studies comparing the operations performed and surgery recommended by doctors who are paid for the operations they do with those performed and recommended by salaried doctors who receive no extra income from surgery.

If these figures seem a bit high, you can have your pick. The figure accepted by Dr. George A. Silver, professor of public health at the Yale University School of Medicine, is 15,000 deaths a year "attributable to unnecessary surgery."[53] Dr. Silver places the annual cost of excess surgery at $4.8 billion.[54] In an article on an experimental program by Blue Cross and Blue Shield aimed at curbing unnecessary surgery, *Newsweek* reports that

a Congressional committee earlier this year [1976] estimated that more than 2 million of the elective operations performed in 1974 were not only unnecessary—but also killed about 12,000 patients and cost nearly $4 billion.[55]

In 1974, the FBI reported that a "knife or other cutting instrument" was the weapon used in 17.6 percent of the 20,600 murders during that year. That works out to 3626 murders due to "cutting or stabbing."[56] Obviously, the FBI does not include the scalpel as a "knife or other cutting instrument." If they did, they would have had to report that between 15,626 and 19,626 persons were killed by "cutting or stabbing" in 1974—depending on whether you take *News-week's* figure or Dr. Wolfe's. No matter how you slice it, the scalpel is more dangerous than the switchblade.

While they are at it, the FBI should probably add the hypodermic needle and the prescription to their list of murder weapons. Professor Silver points out that these are also death-dealing instruments.

> Of the 6 billion doses of antibiotic medicines administered each year by injection or prescription, it is estimated that 22 percent are unnecessary. Of the doses given, 10,000 result in fatal or near-fatal reactions. Somewhere between 2,000 and 10,000 deaths probably would not have occurred if the drugs, meant for the patient's benefit, had not been given.[57]

In fact, if someone had the temerity to publish a *Uniform Crime Reports* that really portrayed the way Americans are murdered, the FBI's statistics on the *type of weapon used* in murder would have to be changed, for 1974, from those shown in Table 2a to those shown in Table 2b.

The figures shown in Table 2b would give American citizens a much more honest picture of what threatens them. We are not likely to see it broadcast by the criminal justice system, however, since it would also give American citizens a more honest picture of *who* threatens them.

We should not leave this topic without noting that the 4 to 5 billion dollars that needless surgery costs far outstrips the 3 to 3.5 billion dollars taken by the thieves the FBI concerns itself with. To this we should add the cost of the unnecessary 22 percent of the 6 billion administered doses of antibiotic medicines. Even at the ridiculously low cost of $2 per dose, this adds $2.6 billion to the loot taken by the hypocritical heirs of Hippocrates.

3. *Waging Chemical Warfare Against America*

> [From] 60 to 90 percent of the more than 365,000 Americans expected to die of cancer this year will have contracted the dis-

Table 2a How Americans Are Murdered

		Murder, Type of Weapon Used[58]		
Total	Firearms	Knife or Other Cutting Instrument	Other Weapon: Club, Poison, etc.	Personal Weapon: Hands, Fists, etc.
20,600	13,987	3,626	1,401	1,586

Table 2b How Americans Are Murdered

			Murder, Type of Weapon Used[59]				
Total	Occupational Hazard	Inadequate Emergency Medical Care	Knife or Other Cutting Instrument Including Scalpel	Firearms	Hypodermic or Prescription	Other Weapon: Club, Poison, etc.	Personal Weapon: Hands, Fists, etc.
168,600	114,000	20,000	15,626	13,987	2,000	1,401	1,586

75

ease from environmental factors, including cigarette smoke
and industrial chemicals, according to the National Cancer
Institute. And the American Cancer Society estimates that one
out of four Americans alive today will ultimately develop some
form of cancer. Many more will die or be seriously disabled by
chemicals which attack the nervous system, the lungs and
other organs.[60]

Environmentally caused cancer is preventable cancer.
This means that a concerted national effort could result in
saving 200,000 or more lives a year and reducing each individual's chances of getting cancer in his or her lifetime to
1-in-8 or less. If you think that this would require a massive
effort in terms of money and personnel, you are right. But
how much of an effort would the nation make to stop a foreign invader who was taking a thousand lives a day in casualties and who was bent on killing one-quarter of the present population?

In the face of this "invasion" which is already underway,
the U.S. government has allocated $760 million to the
National Cancer Institute, and NCI has allocated $48 mil-
lion to the study of the chemical causes of cancer. This is an
amount considerably less than the government spent *per
day* for the Vietnam War at its height! The simple truth is
that the government that strives so mightily to protect us
from a guerrilla war 10,000 miles from home is doing next to
nothing to protect us against the chemical war in our midst.
This war is being waged against us on three fronts:

• Air pollution
• Cigarette smoking
• Food additives

Not only are we losing on all three fronts, but it looks like
we do not even have the will to fight.

In April 1976, Dr. Umberto Saffioti, director of the National Cancer Institute's program of research into the chemical
causes of cancer, resigned to protest three years' lack of support by NCI leaders.[61] In a letter stating his reasons for step-
ping down, he said,

I cannot accept any longer a situation which in fact deprives the regulatory agencies, industry, labor, consumers, and the scientific community of data of urgent public health value: It is people who are now exposed to toxic agents and who are not protected because the necessary support was not provided in time.[62]

Earlier the same year, three lawyers for the Environmental Protection Agency resigned "'because of the continued failure of the EPA to take effective action,' to regulate possible cancer-causing and other toxic chemicals in the air, food supply, drinking water and waterways." In a joint statement, the attorneys said,

It is clear from recent actions that the agency intends to refrain from vigorous enforcement of available toxic-substances controls and to retrench from the few legal precedents which it has set for evaluating the cancer hazards posed by the chemicals.[63]

In testimony before the U.S. Senate Committee on Commerce, Samuel S. Epstein, M.D., Swetland Professor of Environmental Health and Human Ecology, in the Department of Pharmacology of the Case Western Reserve University School of Medicine, said in 1973,

It is preposterous...that [the administration] can recommend a $100 million program for the treatment and prevention of cancer when current FDA [Food and Drug Administration] practice is deliberately allowing an increase in the total burden of carcinogenic elements in our human diet.[64]

The evidence linking *air pollution* and cancer, as well as other serious and often fatal diseases, has been rapidly accumulating in recent years. During 1975, the epidemiological branch of the National Cancer Institute did a massive county-by-county analysis of cancer in the United States, mapping the "cancer hotspots" in the nation. The result was summed up by Dr. Glenn Paulson, assistant commissioner of science in the New Jersey Department of Environmental Protection: "If you know where the chemical industry is, you know where the cancer hotspots are."[65] What distinguishes these findings from the material on occupational hazards discussed above is that NCI investigators found higher death rates for *all* those living in the "cancer hotspots"—not just the workers in the offending plants.

For instance, NCI researchers found that Deer Lodge County in Montana ranked ninth out of 3021 U.S. counties in lung cancer death rates. Deer Lodge County is the home of the Anaconda Company's giant copper-smelting works. The county's death rate was twice the rate expected for a rural county. A study by the Montana Department of Health and Environmental Sciences showed that the county's death rates for emphysema, asthma, and bronchitis are also well above the national average. Another study by two NCI researchers found that in *all* 36 U.S. counties with smelters, the incidence of lung cancer is above the national average. And "the researchers found high lung cancer death rates not only in men—who are often exposed to arsenic on their jobs inside smelters—but also among women who generally never went inside smelters and were not previously believed to have been exposed to arsenic." Explanation: "neighborhood air pollution from industrial sources of inorganic arsenic."[66]

New Jersey, however, took the prize for having the highest cancer death rate in the nation. NCI investigators found that "19 of New Jersey's 21 counties rank in the top 10 percent of all counties in the nation for cancer death rates." Salem County, home of E. I. Du Pont de Nemours and Company's Chambers Works, which has been manufacturing chemicals since 1919, "has the highest bladder cancer death rate in the nation—8.7 deaths per 100,000 persons."[67]

In 1970, Lester B. Lave and Eugene P. Seskin reviewed over 50 scientific studies of the relationship between air pollution and morbidity and mortality rates for lung cancer, nonrespiratory tract cancers, cardiovascular disease, bronchitis, and other respiratory diseases. They found in *every* instance a *positive quantifiable relationship.* Using sophisticated statistical techniques, they concluded that a 50 percent reduction in air pollution in major urban areas would result in:

- A 25 percent reduction in mortality from lung cancer (using 1974 mortality rates, this represents a potential saving of 19,500 lives per year).
- A 25 percent reduction in morbidity and mortality due to respiratory disease (potential saving of 27,000 lives per year).
- A 20 percent reduction in morbidity and mortality due to cardiovascular disease (a potential saving of 252,000 lives per year).[68]

In addition, even a 10 percent reduction in air pollution could could be expected to "decrease the total death rate by 0.5 percent."[69]

And so the chemical air war goes on. No one can deny that we know the enemy. No one can deny that we know the toll it is taking. Indeed, we can compute the number of deaths that result from every day that we refuse to mount an offensive. But refuse we do. And thus for the time being the only advice we can offer someone who values his life, is: If you must breathe our air, don't inhale.

The evidence linking *cigarette smoking* and cancer is overwhelming and need not be repeated here. It should be noted, however, that according to figures reported by Dr. Marvin A. Schneiderman of the National Cancer Institute, of the 80,000 deaths from lung and larynx cancer expected for 1974, about 70,000 could be prevented by means currently at our disposal—primarily by eliminating cigarette smoking.[70] This is enough to expose the hypocrisy of running a full-scale war against heroin (which produces no degenerative disease) while allowing cigarette sales and advertising to flourish. It should also be enough to underscore the point that once again there are threats to our lives much greater than criminal homicide. And the legal order does not protect us against them.

Having advocated the legalization of heroin in Chapter 1, I do not intend to argue for the criminalization of tobacco in Chapter 2. It should be said, however, that the heroin and cigarette issues are not strictly parallel. Making the sale and possession of cigarettes illegal (or even taxing cigarettes prohibitively, so that the price of a pack of cigarettes would be, say, $5, instead of $.50[71]) could save many more lives a year than the whole criminal justice effort, including the "war" on heroin, currently does. I will stand, however, by the age-old liberal principle that in a free society each individual should be allowed to go to hell by a route of his choosing.

However, it is no violation of this principle to use the law to protect people who are endangered by tobacco and who have not freely chosen to subject themselves to that danger. In this light, there is growing evidence of high cancer rates among "passive smokers"—people who are regularly in the vicinity of smokers. As this evidence accumulates there will be increasing justification to protect nonsmokers from smokers by legally mandating smoke-free zones in airplanes, restaurants, offices, and so on. More immediate, however, is the case of the teenage smoker.

The law has regularly been used to protect people from their own "choices" when they are either subject to undue pressure or too young to make a sound choice (i.e., below the "age of consent"). I think both conditions obtain for teenage smokers in the United States. They find themselves in a period of maximum awkwardness, with little support from the adult world they are struggling to enter. They reach out, almost involuntarily, for a crutch, a prop, a mark of *savoir faire*. And magazine advertisements, coupled with TV and film images, offer them what they think they need: the cigarette erotically inhaled by healthy, sexy, fashionable men and women or casually drooping (Bogart-style) from the cool tough hero's lips.

And they take it. In fact, in the years since the surgeon general's report officially linked cancer and cigarettes, even in the years since 1970, when cigarette ads were taken off TV and radio, smoking among high school youngsters has been increasing rapidly. One study published in the *American Journal of Public Health* calls the growth of smoking among students in grades 7 through 12 an *epidemic*.[72] And "people who start smoking at age 15 are five times more likely to die of lung cancer than those who start at 25"![73]

Today, more money is being spent advertising cigarettes in newspapers and magazines and on billboards than was spent on *all* cigarette advertising during the last year that TV and radio advertising was allowed.[74] And these advertisers are getting their money's worth. Cigarette sales are up 30 percent since 1969.[75] In other words, *a multibillion dollar industry that thrives on hooking people to a known killer is allowed not only to flourish but also to advertise its deadly wares*. Certainly, it is time to forbid *all* advertising of tobacco products and to consider drastically restricting the use of cigarettes in all media presentations. Until that time we are accomplices in yet another massive assault on the lives and well-being of American citizens.

The average American consumes *one pound* of chemical *food additives* per year.[76] Speaking on the floor of the United States Senate in 1972, Senator Gaylord Nelson said,

> People are finally waking up to the fact that the average American daily diet is substantially adulterated with unnecessary and poisonous chemicals and frequently filled with neutral, nonnutritious substances. We are being chemically medicated against our will and cheated of food value by low nutrition foods.[77]

The case against food additives cannot be made as precisely as that against pollution and cigarettes. In fact, that is part of the case! That is, a hard look at the chemicals we eat and at the federal agency that is empowered to protect us against eating dangerous chemicals reveals the striking lack of evidence and thus the recklessness with which we are being "medicated against our will."

Beatrice Hunter has taken such a hard look and reports her findings in a book aptly titled, *The Mirage of Safety*. Her book is a catalogue of the possible dangers that lurk in the foods we eat. But more than this, it is a description of how the Food and Drug Administration, through a combination of

lax enforcement and uncritical acceptance of the results of
the food industry's own "scientific" research, has allowed a
situation to exist in which the American food-eating public is
the real guinea pig for nearly *three thousand* food additives.
As a result, we are subjected to chemicals that are strongly
suspected of producing cancer,[78] gallbladder ailments,[79]
hyperkinesis in children,[80] and allergies[81]; to others that
inhibit "mammalian cell growth" and "may adversely affect
the rate of DNA, RNA, and protein synthesis"[82]; and to still
others that are capable of crossing the placental barrier between mother and fetus and are suspected causes of birth defects and congenital diseases.[83]

In view of the fact that "one out of every five to ten people
has a major allergy of disabling proportions and consequences"[84] and that between "4 to 7.5 percent of human
deliveries yield individuals that have developmental defects
that will interfere with survival or result in clinical disease
before the end of the first year of life,"[85] coupled with what
we already know about the role of external chemicals in the
causation of cancer, to call government and industry practices reckless is mild. What we have is a callous policy that
amounts to subjecting the food-eating public to unknown but
reasonably suspected risks to their lives and well-being in
the name of food industry profits. It is in this light that our
lack of precise knowledge of the consequences of our chemical diet is itself proof of the recklessness of present practices.

Based on the knowledge we do have, there can be no doubt
that air pollution, tobacco, and food additives amount to a
chemical war that makes the crime wave look like a football
scrimmage. Quite conservatively, I think we can estimate
the death toll in this war as at least a quarter of a million
lives a year—*more than twelve times the number killed by
criminal homicide!*

4. Poverty Kills

We are long passed the day when we could believe that poverty was caused by forces outside human control. Poverty is

"caused" by lack of money, which means that once a society reaches a level of prosperity at which many enjoy a relatively high standard of living, then poverty can be eliminated or at least significantly reduced by transferring some of what the "haves" have to the "have-nots." In other words, regardless of what caused poverty in the past, what causes it to continue in the present is the refusal of those who have more to share with those who have less. Now you may think these remarks trite or naive. But they are not offered as an argument for redistribution of income, although I think such a redistribution is long overdue. These remarks are presented to make a much simpler point, which is that poverty exists in a wealthy society like our own *because we allow it to exist.* And, therefore, we[86] share responsibility for poverty and for its consequences.

We are prone to think that the consequences of poverty are fairly straightforward: less money = less things. And so poor people have fewer clothes or cars or appliances, go to the theater less often, and live in smaller homes with less or cheaper furniture. And this is true, and sad, but perhaps not intolerable. I will argue that one of the things poor people have less of is *good health.* Less money means less nutritious food, less heat in winter, less fresh air in summer, less distance from other sick people, less knowledge about illness or medicine, fewer doctor visits, fewer dental visits, less preventive health care, and above all, less first-quality medical attention when all these other deprivations take their toll and a poor person finds himself seriously ill. What this means is that the poor suffer more from poor health and die earlier, than do those who are well off. Poverty robs them of their days while they are alive and then kills them before their time. A prosperous society that allows poverty in its midst is guilty of murder.

William Ryan writes in his book *Blaming the Victim,*

Our health problems are concentrated among the poor. In New York City, the central Harlem health district reports an infant mortality rate of 49.5 per thousand while the well-to-do district of Kips Bay-Yorkville has a rate of only 14.7 per thousand. According to the American Public Health Association, poor fam-

ilies suffer from disabling heart disease three times more frequently than others; and from visual impairment, seven times
more frequently. A study of Head Start children in Boston revealed that almost one in three had major undiscovered health
problems. The statistics can be cited almost indefinitely, and
they add up to a formulation that is wearingly familiar—the
poor man and the black man suffer and end up with the lowest
health status.[87]

In the 1960s, a study was done in Chicago comparing
health in the poor areas of the city with health in the
wealthier areas.[88] The study found that

the overall *mortality* rate in poverty areas was 40 percent
higher than in nonpoverty areas. With respect to *infant mortality* rates, the measure used worldwide as a general indicator
of community health, poverty areas exceeded nonpoverty
areas by 75 percent. In a measure that many students consider
to be an even better and more sensitive indicator of community
health, the *post-neonatal mortality* rate (deaths among infants
who survive the first month of life) for poverty areas exceeded
nonpoverty areas by 100 percent.[89]

A review of over 30 historical and contemporary studies of
the relationship of economic class and life expectancy af-
firms the obvious conclusion that "class influences one's
chances of staying alive. Almost without exception, the evidence shows that classes differ on mortality rates."[90] An
article in the July 1976 issue of the *American Journal of
Epidemiology* states that a "vast body of evidence has
shown consistently that those in the lower classes have
higher mortality, morbidity, and disability rates" and that
these "are in part due to inadequate medical care services as
well as to the impact of a toxic and hazardous physical
environment."[91]

A comparison of the health and mortality of blacks and
whites in America yields insight into the relationship of
health and mortality to economic class. In 1974, about 1 out
of every 3 blacks lived below the poverty or low-income level,
as compared to 1 out of every 11 whites.[92] Median income of

black families in 1973 and 1974 was 58 percent (slightly less than *three-fifths!*) of the median income of white families. And this represents a loss of ground compared to the years 1967 through 1972, when median black family income hovered between 59 and 61 percent of the median for whites.[93] For these reasons, it is generally a safe bet to assume that data on the lives of blacks in America are also data on the impact of low economic status in America.

In 1973, black mothers died in childbirth at a rate *three times* that of white mothers. Black infant mortality was two-thirds higher than white (17.9 per 1000 live births to 11.8), and the black postneonatal mortality rate was 8.3 per 1000 live births, as compared to 4 per 1000 live white births. This means that black mothers lost their infants between the ages of 1 month to 11 months as a rate *more than twice* that for whites![94]

Life expectancy figures paint the most tragic picture of all. As of 1973, a newly born black male could expect to live 61.9 years, while a newly born white male could look forward to 68.4 years. A newly born black female could expect to live 70.1 years, as compared to 76.1 for a white female. In other words, a black man could expect six and one-half fewer years of life than a white man, and a black woman could expect six fewer years of life than a white woman![95]

Now life expectancy figures are averages; some people live longer and some live shorter. And, of course, some blacks live longer than some whites. But however individuals fare, the figures indicate that blacks are cheated out of a considerable number of years of life—enough to average out to six lost years per person. In other words, for any hundred black men, we can assume that they share between them 6190 years of life, while 100 white men have 6840 years to divide among themselves. Now there is no reason to assume that life expectancy is significantly affected by racial or genetic factors.[96] This means that we can assume that the life expectancy of white Americans is the minimum that any American should expect[97] and thus that the various indignities that go with being black in America are responsible for much if not all the discrepancy between black and white life expectancy rates. Of these various indignities, low economic status is surely the prime cause of poor health and early death, since access to money could undoubtedly do much to overcome the other effects of racism on health.

From this, an inescapable conclusion follows. If we assume that in the absence of poverty, blacks would have about the same life expectancy as whites, then poverty robs every black person of six years of life, on the average. _Poverty kills_. And a society that could remedy its poverty but does not is an accomplice in murder.

* * *

Once again, our investigations lead to the same result. The criminal justice system does not protect us against the gravest threats to life, limb, or possessions. Its definitions of crime are not simply a reflection of the objective dangers that threaten us. The workplace, the medical profession, the air we breathe, and the poverty we refuse to rectify lead to far more human suffering, far more death and disability, and take far more dollars from our pockets than the murders, aggravated assaults, and thefts reported annually by the FBI. And what is more, this human suffering is preventable. A government really intent on protecting our well-being could enforce work safety regulations, police the medical profession, require that clean air standards be met, and funnel sufficient money to the poor to alleviate the major disabilities of poverty. But it does not. Instead we hear a lot of cant about law and order and a lot of rant about crime in the streets. It is as if our leaders were not only refusing to protect us from the major threats to our well-being but trying to cover up this refusal by diverting our attention to crime—as if this were the real threat. But as we have seen, the criminal justice system is a carnival mirror that presents a distorted image of what threatens us. And the distortions do not end with the definitions of crime. As we shall see in what follows, new distortions enter at every level of the system, so that in the end, when we look in our prisons to see who really threatens us, all we see are poor people. By that time, virtually all the well-to-do people who endanger us have been discreetly weeded out of the system. As we watch this process unfold in the following chapter, we should bear in mind the conclusion of the present chapter: all the mechanisms by which the criminal justice system comes down more frequently and more harshly on the poor criminal than on the well-off criminal take place *after* most of the dangerous acts of the well-to-do have been excluded from the definition of crime itself. The bias against the poor within the criminal justice system is all the more striking when we recognize that the door to that system is shaped in a way that excludes in advance the most dangerous acts of the well-to-do. Demonstrating this has been the purpose of the present chapter.

Footnotes

1. *The Washigton Star*, March 14, 1976, pp. A-1, A-9.
2. Ibid., p. A-9.
3. Gerald R. Ford, president of the United States, "To Insure Domestic Tranquility: Mandatory Sentence for Convicted Felons," speech delivered at the Yale Law School Sesquicentennial Convocation, New Haven, Connecticut, April 25, 1975, in *Vital Speeches of the Day*, XXXXI, No. 15 (May 15, 1975), p. 451.
4. *The Washington Post*, September 16, 1975, p. C1.
5. Ibid.; see also The Maryland-National Capital Parks and Planning Commission, *Crime Analysis 1975: Prince George's County* (August 1975), p. 86.
6. *UCR-1974*, p. 186.
7. *The Washington Post*, September 16, 1975, p. C1; and *Crime Analysis 1975: Prince George's County* (August 1975), p. 86.
8. *UCR-1974*, p. 191.
9. Out of 1,289,524 persons arrested for FBI Index Crimes in 1974, 1,043,155, or over 80 percent were males. See *UCR-1974*, p. 190. In Prince George's County, males "represented three of every four serious crime defendants." *Crime Analysis 1975: Prince George's County*, p. 3.
10. Out of 1,474,427 persons arrested for FBI Index Crimes in 1974,

1,267,955 were "city arrests" and 420,682 were "suburban"
(suburban arrest figures include arrests in suburban cities,
and thus overlap with statistics for city arrests). *UCR-1974*,
p. 180.

11. Jeffrie G. Murphy, "Marxism and Retribution," *Philosophy &
Public Affairs*, 2, No. 3 (Spring 1973), p. 237. Cf. Samuel Jor-
dan, "Prison Reform: In Whose Interest?" *Criminal Law Bul-
letin*, 7, No. 9 (November 1971), pp. 779-787: "Of the 1.2 million
criminal offenders handled each day by some part of the
United States correctional system, 80 percent are members of
the lowest 12 percent income group—or black and poor,"
quoted in Jessica Mitford, *Kind and Usual Punishment* (New
York: Alfred A. Knopf, 1973), p. 289.

12. *Challenge*, p. 44; see also p. 160.

13. John N. Mitchell, "Crime Prevention: Citizen Participation,"
speech delivered before the Conference on Crime and the
Urban Crisis of the National Emergency Committee of the
National Council on Crime and Delinquency, San Francisco,
California, February 3, 1969, in *Vital Speeches of the Day*,
XXXV, No. 10 (March 1, 1969), p. 290.

14. See footnote 3, above.

15. See footnote 12, above.

16. This transformation has been noted by Erving Goffman in his
sensitive description of total institutions, *Asylums* (Garden
City, New York: Doubleday, 1961):

> The interpretative scheme of the total institution auto-
> matically begins to operate as soon as the inmate enters,
> the staff having the notion that entrance is *prima facie*
> evidence that one must be the kind of person the institu-
> tion was set up to handle. A man in a political prison must
> be traitorous; a man in a prison must be a law-breaker; a
> man in a mental hospital must be sick. If not traitorous,
> criminal, or sick, why else would he be there? (p. 84)

So too, a person who calls forth the society's most drastic
weapons of defense must pose the gravest danger to its well-
being. Why else the reaction? The point is put well and tersely
by D. Chapman: "There is a circular pattern in thinking: we
are hostile to wicked people, wicked people are punished, punished people are wicked, we are hostile to punished people
because they are wicked." "The Stereotype of the Criminal and

the Social Consequences," *International Journal of Criminology and Penology*, 1 (1973), p. 16.

17. Richard Quinney, *The Social Reality of Crime* (Boston: Little, Brown, 1970). In his later work, for example, *Critique of Legal Order: Crime Control in Capitalist Society* (Boston: Little, Brown, 1973), and *Class, State & Crime* (New York: McKay, 1977), Quinney moves clearly into a Marxist problematic and his conclusions dovetail with many in this book. In my own view, however, Quinney has not yet accomplished a satisfactory synthesis between the "social reality" theory and his later Marxism. Elsewhere, I have examined Quinney's theory from the standpoint of moral philosophy. See Jeffrey H. Reiman, "Doing Justice to Criminology: Reflections on the Implications for Criminology of Recent Developments in the Philosophy of Justice," in *Issues in Criminal Justice: Planning and Evaluation*, eds., Marc Riedel and Duncan Chappell (New York: Praeger, 1976), pp. 134-142.

18. *Social Reality of Crime*, p. 15.

19. Sir James Fitzjames Stephen, from his *History of the Criminal Law of England*, II (1883), excerpted in *Crime, Law and Society*, eds., Abraham S. Goldstein and Joseph Goldstein (New York: The Free Press, 1971), p. 21.

20. Troy Duster, *The Legislation of Morality: Law, Drugs, and Moral Judgment* (New York: The Free Press, 1970), pp. 3-76.

21. Norval Morris and Gordon Hawkins, *The Honest Politician's Guide to Crime Control* (Chicago: The University of Chicago Press, 1970), p. 2.

22. *Challenge*, p. 7.

23. *UCR-1974*, p. 55 and p. 6. For 1976, murders and nonnegligent manslaughters were down to 18,780, aggravated assaults rose to 490,850, and forcible rapes rose slightly to 56,730. *UCR-1976*, p. 37.

24. *UCR-1974*, p. 178. Because of widespread underreporting of larceny, this figure certainly underestimates the real value of stolen property. Since our purpose here is to demonstrate bias in the definition of crime, it suffices to use figures for reported larceny, since this is the information upon which criminal justice policy decisions are based.

25. See David Wise, *The Politics of Lying: Government Deception, Secrecy and Power* (New York: Vintage Books, 1973), pp. 61-67.

26. *The President's Report on Occupational Safety and Health* (Washington, D.C: U. S. Government Printing Office, 1972).

27. See, for instance, Joseph A. Page and Mary-Win O'Brien, *Bitter Wages: Ralph Nader's Study Group Report on Disease and Injury on the Job* (New York: Grossman, 1973); Rachel Scott, *Muscle and Blood* (New York: E. P. Dutton, 1974); and Jeanne M. Stellman and Susan M. Daum, *Work Is Dangerous to Your Health* (New York: Vintage Books, 1973). See also Fran Lynn, "The Dust in Willie's Lungs," *The Nation*, 222, No. 7 (February 21, 1976), pp. 209-212; and Joel Swartz, "Silent Killers at Work," *Crime and Social Justice*, 3 (Summer 1975), pp. 15-20.
28. *President's Report on Occupational Safety and Health*, p. 111.
29. *UCR-1974*, p. 55.
30. Susan Q. Stranahan, "Why 115,000 Workers Will Die This Year," *Boston Sunday Globe*, March 21, 1976, p. A4.
31. *Accident Facts*, National Safety Council (1971 ed.), pp. 3, 5, 23-24; cited in Page and O'Brien, *Bitter Wages*, p. 161.
32. Steve Turner, "Work Can Be Dangerous to Your Health," *Boston Sunday Globe*, May 2, 1976, p. 14.
33. *UCR-1974*, p. 9. This had slowed to one murder every 28 minutes in 1976. *UCR-1976*, p. 6.
34. Page and O'Brien, *Bitter Wages*, p. 16.
35. Ibid., p. 18.
36. Ibid., p. 23; and Scott, *Muscle and Blood*, p. 196.
37. Scott, pp. 45-46; cf. Page and O'Brien, p. 25.
38. Page and O'Brien, p. 37.
39. Ibid., p. 45.
40. Stranahan, "Why 115,000 Workers Will Die This Year," p. A1.
41. The quotations in this paragraph are from Stranahan, p. A4.
42. Swartz, "Silent Killers at Work," p. 18. On the average fine, Rachel Scott sets it at "a trifling twenty-five dollars per violation" in 1972. *Muscle and Blood*, p. 287. Referring to more recent practices, Susan Stranahan cites a study that found the average fine actually levied to be $25.87. "Why 115,000 Workers Will Die This Year," p. A4.
43. Page and O'Brien, *Bitter Wages*, p. 71.
44. Ibid., p. 74. (Emphasis added.)
45. Scott, *Muscle and Blood*, pp. 35-36.
46. Ibid., pp. 109, 111.
47. Ibid., p. 112.
48. Page and O'Brien, *Bitter Wages*, p. 73.
49. Ibid., p. 73.
50. Scott, p. 239.
51. *Challenge*, p. 52. (Emphasis added.) See also p. 3 for then-

prevailing homicide rates.

52. *The Washington Post*, July 16, 1975, p. A3.
53. George A. Silver, M.D., "The Medical Insurance Disease," *The Nation*, 222, No. 12 (March 27, 1976), p. 369.
54. Ibid., p. 371.
55. *Newsweek*, March 29, 1976, p. 67. Lest anyone think this is a new problem, compare this passage written in a popular magazine about 25 years ago:

> In an editorial on medical abuses, the *Journal of the Medical Association of Georgia* referred to "surgeons who paradoxically are often cast in the role of the supreme hero by the patient and family and at the same time may be doing the greatest amount of harm to the individual."
> Unnecessary operations on women, stemming from the combination of a trusting patient and a split fee, have been so deplored by honest doctors that the phrase "rape of the pelvis" has been used to describe them. The American College of Surgeons, impassioned foe of fee-splitting, has denounced unnecessary hysterectomies, uterine suspensions, Caesarian sections. [Howard Whitman, "Why Some Doctors Should Be in Jail," *Colliers*, October 30, 1953, p. 24.]

56. *UCR-1974*, p. 18.
57. Silver, p. 369. Silver's estimates are extremely conservative. Some studies suggest that between 30,000 and 160,000 individuals die as a result of drugs prescribed by their doctors. See Boyce Rensberger, "Thousands a Year Killed by Faulty Prescriptions," *The New York Times*, January 28, 1976, pp. 1, 17. If we assume, with Silver, that at least 20 percent are unnecessary, then this puts the annual death toll from unnecessary prescriptions at between 6000 and 32,000 persons. For an in-depth look at the recklessness with which prescription drugs are put on the market and the laxness with which the Food and Drug Administration exercises its mandate to protect the public, see the series of eight articles by Morton Mintz, "The Medicine Business," in *The Washington Post*, June 27, 28, 29, 30, July 1, 2, 3, 4, 1976.
58. Numbers of cases have been computed from percentages in the chart "Murder, Type of Weapon Used, 1969-1974," *UCR-1974*, p. 18.

59. Numbers of cases have been computed by adding in the more conservative of the figures mentioned in the present and previous sections, with those computed from the chart "Murder, Type of Weapon Used, 1969-1974," *UCR-1974*, p. 18.
60. Stephen D. Solomon and Willard S. Randall, "Don't Breathe on the Job," *The Nation*, 222, No. 20 (May 22, 1976), p. 627. Estimates of the percent of cancers caused by external factors vary, but all seem to be between 60 and 90 percent. For instance, Christine Russell writes that

> international experts convened under the auspices of the World Health Organization speculated in 1964 that "extrinsic factors," account for more than 75 percent of human cancers. ["The New War on Cancer, Part I: We're Caught in a Grim Game of Chemical Roulette," *The Washington Star*, May 23, 1976, p. A-10.]

And Beatrice Hunter writes that

> most cancerologists agree that about 80 percent of all human cancers could be prevented if all contact with known exogenous (i.e. having a cause external to the body) carcinogens could be avoided. [*The Mirage of Safety* (New York: Charles Scribner's Sons, 1975), p. 149.]

61. Morton Mintz, "Cancer Scientist Quits in Policy Split," *The Washington Post*, April 30, 1976, p. A2.
62. "The New War on Cancer, Part I," *The Washington Star*, May 23, 1976, p. A-10.
63. Morton Mintz, "3 Lawyers Leave EPA in Protest," *The Washington Post*, February 6, 1976, p. A1. The three lawyers are Jeffrey H. Howard, Frank J. Sizemore III, and William E. Reukauf. All were assigned to regulation of pesticides and toxic substances.
64. Quoted in Hunter, *The Mirage of Safety*, p. 147.
65. Quoted in Stuart Auerbach, "N.J.'s Chemical Belt Takes Its Toll: $4 Billion Industry Tied to Nation's Highest Cancer Death Rate," *The Washington Post*, February 8, 1976, p. A1.
66. Bill Richards, "Arsenic: A Dark Cloud Over 'Big Sky Country,'" *The Washington Post*, February 3, 1976, pp. A1, A5.
67. Quotations in this paragraph are from "N.J.'s Chemical Belt Takes Its Toll," *The Washington Post*, February 8, 1976, p. A1.

68. Lester B. Lave and Eugene P. Seskin, "Air Pollution and Human Health," *Science*, 169, No. 3947 (August 21, 1970), pp. 723-733, especially p. 730. The source for the 1974 mortality rates for lung cancer, respiratory disease (excluding cancer), and cardiovascular disease is the Department of Health, Education and Welfare.

69. Lave and Seskin, p. 728.

70. "The New War on Cancer, Part I," *The Washington Star*, May 23, 1976, p. A-10.

71. It is not immediately evident whether this would be more unfair to the rich or the poor. In any event, it is put forth here simply to illustrate the inconsistency in our policies on tobacco and heroin, not as a serious proposal.

72. Saul R. Kelson, James L. Pullella, and Anders Otterland, "The Growing Epidemic: A Survey of Smoking Habits and Attitudes Toward Smoking Among Students in Grades 7 Through 12 in Toledo and Lucas County (Ohio) Public Schools, 1964-1971," *The American Journal of Public Health*, 65, No. 9 (September, 1975), pp. 923-938; cited in James Fallows "Cigarettes: A Menace We Love to Ignore; Bankrupt Policies, Public and Private," *The Washington Star*, February 29, 1976, p. E-4.

73. Fallows, p. E-4.

74. Ibid., p. E-4.

75. Ibid., p. E-1.

76. Hunter, *The Mirage of Safety*, p. 4.

77. Quoted in Hunter, p. 2.

78. Hunter, pp. 40-41, 64-65, 85, 148-151, *inter alia*.

79. Ibid., p. 119.

80. Ibid., pp. 123-124.

81. Ibid., pp. 127-140.

82. Ibid., pp. 102-103.

83. Ibid., pp. 162-176.

84. Ibid., p. 128. The National Institute of Allergy and Infectious Diseases reports that 17 out of every 100 persons suffers from a major allergy.

85. Hunter, p. 162.

86. At the very least, "we" includes all those who earn considerably above the median income for the nation (around $13,000 for a family in 1974) and who resist, or vote for candidates who resist, moves to redistribute income significantly.

87. William Ryan, *Blaming the Victim* (New York: Random House, 1971), p. 162.

88. Monroe Lerner, "Social Differences in Physical Health," in
    Poverty and Health: A Sociological Analysis, eds., John Kosa
    et al. (Cambridge: Harvard University Press, 1969); cited in
    Edward S. Greenberg, *Serving the Few: Corporate Capitalism
    and the Bias of Government Policy* (New York: John Wiley &
    Sons, 1974), p. 156.
89. Greenberg, *Serving the Few*, p. 156.
90. Aaron Antonovsky, "Class and the Chance for Life," in *Inequality and Justice*, ed., Lee Rainwater (Chicago: Aldine Publishing Co., 1974), p. 177.
91. S. Leonard Syme and Lisa F. Berkman, "Social Class, Susceptibility and Sickness," *American Journal of Epidemiology*,
    104, No. 1 (July, 1976), pp. 1, 4.
92. *Black Population in the U.S.*, p. 41.
93. Ibid., p. 25.
94. Ibid., p. 126.
95. Ibid., p. 123. This difference cannot be explained by the higher
    rate of death by homicide among blacks, since homicide is responsible for only 6 percent of the deaths of black males and
    less than 2 percent of the deaths of black females. Ibid., p. 125.
96. Richard Allen Williams, M.D., reports that "there is no reason
    why the life span of the White should differ from that of the
    Black," in his *Textbook of Black-Related Diseases* (New York:
    McGraw-Hill, 1975), p. 2.
97. This is indeed a minimum, since the level of health for whites
    in America comes nowhere near our technological potential.
    "We rank only 15th in the world in infant mortality, and only
    16th in average life expectancy. Twenty countries have less
    heart disease, and 12 have fewer cases of ulcers, diabetes,
    cirrhosis of the liver, and hypertension. Deaths among women
    in childbirth exceed that of 106 other countries." Greenberg,
    Serving the Few, pp. 154-155. What this means is that the case
    that I have been making that poverty kills blacks an average
    of six years before their time is a conservative one arrived at by
    comparing black life expectancy with white. However, if we
    compared American life expectancy with that of, say, Sweden,
    it could be argued that Americans of all races die before they
    would if we provided them the health care that we are capable
    of providing.

3

The Rich Get Richer and the Poor Get Prison

*When we come to make an intelligent
study of the prison at first hand . . . we are
bound to conclude that after all it is not
so much crime in its general sense that is
penalized, but that it is poverty which
is punished . . .*

*Take a census of the average prison and
you will find that a large majority of
people are there not so much because of
the particular crime they are alleged to
have committed, but for the reason that
they are poor and . . . lacked the money to
engage the services of first class and
influential lawyers.*

Eugene V. Debs, *Walls and Bars*

a. Weeding Out the Wealthy

The offender at the end of the road in prison is likely to be a
member of the lowest social and economic groups in the
country.[1]

This statement in the *Report of the President's Commission on Law Enforcement and Administration of Justice*

is as true today as it was a decade ago when it was written.
Our prisons are indeed, as Ronald Goldfarb has called them,
the National Poorhouse.[2] To most citizens this comes as no
surprise—recall the Typical Criminal and the Typical Crime.
Dangerous crimes, they think, are mainly committed by poor
people. And seeing that prison populations are made up
primarily of the poor only makes them surer of this. They
think, in other words, that the criminal justice system gives a
true reflection of the dangers that threaten them.

On my view, it also comes as no surprise that our prisons
and jails predominantly confine the poor. But this is not
because these are the individuals who most threaten us.
Instead, it is because the criminal justice system effectively
weeds out the well-to-do, so that indeed by the time we reach
the end of the road in prison, the vast majority of those we
find there come from the lower classes. This "weeding out"
process starts before the agents of law enforcement go into
action. In the last chapter, I argued that our very definition
of crime *excludes* a wide variety of actions at least as
dangerous as those included and often worse. Is it any
accident that the kinds of dangerous actions excluded are the
kinds most likely to be performed by the affluent in America?
Even before we mobilize our troops in the war on crime, we
have already guaranteed that large numbers of upper-class
individuals will never come within their sights.

But this process does not stop here. It continues throughout
the criminal justice system. At each level, from arrest to
sentencing, the likelihood of being ignored or released or
lightly treated by the system is greater the better off one is
economically. As the late U.S. Senator Philip Hart has
written,

> Justice has two transmission belts, one for the rich and one for
> the poor. The low-income transmission belt is easier to ride
> without falling off and it gets to prison in shorter order.
>   The transmission belt for the affluent is a little slower and it
> passes innumerable stations where exits are temptingly
> convenient.[3]

What this means is that the criminal justice system functions from start to finish in a way that makes certain that "the offender at the end of the road in prison is likely to be a member of the lowest social and economic groups in the country."

For the same criminal behavior, the poor are more likely to be arrested; if arrested, they are more likely to be charged; if charged, more likely to be convicted; if convicted, more likely to be sentenced to prison; and if sentenced, more likely to be given longer prison terms than members of the middle and upper classes.[4] In other words, the image of the criminal population one sees in our nation's jails and prisons is an image distorted by the shape of the criminal justice system itself. It is the face of evil reflected in a carnival mirror, but it is no laughing matter.

The face in the criminal justice carnival mirror is also, as we have already noted, very frequently a black face. Although blacks do not comprise the majority of the inmates in our jails and prisons, they make up a proportion that far outstrips their proportion in the population.[5] But here, too, the image we see is distorted by the processes of the criminal justice system itself. Edwin Sutherland and Donald Cressey write, in their widely used textbook, *Criminology*, that

> numerous studies have shown that African-Americans are more likely to be arrested, indicted, convicted, and committed to an institution than are whites who commit the same offenses, and many other studies have shown that blacks have a poorer chance than whites to receive probation, a suspended sentence, parole, commutation of a death sentence, or pardon.[6]

There can be little doubt that the criminal justice process is distorted by racism as well as by economic bias.[7] Nevertheless, it does not pay to look at these as two independent forms of bias. It is my view that, at least as far as criminal justice is concerned, racism is simply one powerful form of economic bias. And I shall use evidence on differential treatment of

blacks as evidence of differential treatment of members of
the lower-classes. There are five reasons for this.

1. First and foremost, black Americans are disproportion-
    ately poor. Nearly *one-third* of all black Americans were
    below the poverty or low-income level in 1974, as com-
    pared to about *one-eleventh* of white Americans.
2. Blacks who travel the full route of the criminal justice
    system and end up in jail or prison are nearly identical
    in economic condition to whites who do. For example,
    in 1972, 47 percent of black jail inmates and 43 percent of
    white jail inmates had prearrest annual incomes of less
    than $2000.[8]
3. The factors that are most likely to keep one out of trouble
    with the law and out of prison, such as a suburban living
    room instead of a tenement alley to gamble in or legal
    counsel able to devote time to one's case instead of an
    overburdened public defender, are the kinds of things
    that money can buy, regardless of race, creed, or national
    origin.
4. Curiously enough, statistics on differential treatment of
    races are available in greater abundance than are statis-
    tics on differential treatment of economic classes. For
    instance, although the FBI tabulates arrest rates by race
    (as well as by sex, age, and geographical area), it omits
    class or income. Similarly, both the President's Crime
    Commission Report and Sutherland and Cressey's *Crim-
    inology* have index entries for race or racial discrimina-
    tion but none for class or income of offenders. It would
    seem that both independent and government data gath-
    erers are more willing to own up to America's racism
    than to its class bias.
5. Finally, it is my belief that the economic powers-that-be
    in America have sufficient power to end or drastically
    reduce racist bias in the criminal justice system. To the
    extent that they allow it to exist, it is not unreasonable
    to assume that it furthers their economic interests.

For all these reasons, racism will be treated here as either a form of economic bias or a tool that achieves the same end.

In the remainder of this chapter, I will try to show how the criminal justice system functions to *weed out the wealthy* (meaning both middle- and upper-class offenders) at each stage of the process and thus produces a distorted image of the crime problem. Before entering into this discussion, two provisos should be noted. First, it is not my view that the poor are all innocent victims persecuted by the evil rich. The poor do commit crimes, and my own assumption is that the vast majority of the poor who are confined in our prisons are guilty of the crimes for which they were sentenced. In addition, there is good evidence that the poor do commit a greater portion of the crimes against person and property listed in the FBI Index than the middle and upper classes do, relative to their numbers in the national population. What I have already tried to prove is that the crimes in the FBI Index are not the acts that threaten us most, and what I will try to prove in what follows is that the poor are arrested and punished by the criminal justice system much more frequently than their contribution to the crime problem would warrant—and thus the criminals who populate our prisons as well as the public's imagination are predominantly poor.

The second proviso is this. The following discussion has been divided into three sections that correspond to the major criminal justice decision points and that also correspond to hypotheses two, three, and four which were set out on page 56. As always, such classifications are a bit neater than reality, and so they should not be taken as rigid compartments. Many of the distorting processes operate at all criminal justice decision points. So, for example, while I shall primarily discuss the light-handed treatment of white-collar criminals in the section on sentencing, it is also true that white-collar criminals are less likely to be arrested, or charged, or convicted than are criminals with collars of other colors. The section in which a given issue will be treated is a reflection of the point in the criminal justice process at which the disparities are most striking. Suffice it to say, however, that the disparities between the treatment of the poor and the nonpoor are to be found at all points of the process.

1. Arrest

The problem with most official records of who commits crime is that they are really statistics on who gets arrested and convicted. If, as I will show, the police are more likely to arrest some people tha.. others, these official statistics may tell us more about police tnan about criminals. In any event, they give us little reliable data about those who commit crime and do not get caught. Some social scientists, suspicious of the bias built into official records, have tried to devise other methods of determining who has committed a crime. Most often, these methods involve an interview or questionnaire in which the respondent is assured of anonymity and asked to reveal whether or not he has committed any offenses for which he could be arrested and convicted. Techniques to check reliability of these self-reports have also been devised; however, if their reliability is still in doubt, common sense would dictate that they would understate rather than over-state the number of individuals who have committed crimes and never come to official notice. In light of this, the con-clusions of these studies are rather astounding. It would seem that crime is the national pastime. *Everybody does it*!

The President's Crime Commission conducted a survey of 10,000 households and discovered that "91 percent of all Americans have violated laws that could have subjected them to a term of imprisonment at one time in their lives."[9] They also report the findings of a study of 1690 persons (1020 males, 670 females) mostly from the state of New York. Asked which of 49 felonies and misdemeanors (excluding traffic offenses) they had committed,

Ninety-one percent of the respondents admitted they had committed one or more offenses for which they might have received jail or prison sentences. Thirteen percent of the males admitted to grand larceny, 26 percent to auto theft, and 17 percent to burglary. *Sixty-four percent of the males and 27 percent of the females committed at least one felony for which they had not been apprehended.*[10]

Keep in mind that a felony is a crime for which an individual can serve one or more years in prison and that many of the individuals now in jail are there only for misdemeanors!

A number of other studies bear out the conclusion that serious criminal behavior is widespread among middle- and upper-class individuals, although these individuals are rarely, if ever, arrested. Some of the studies show that there are no significant differences between economic classes in the incidence of criminal behavior.[11] Others conclude that while lower-class individuals do commit more than their share of crime, arrest records overstate their share and understate that of the middle and upper classes.[12]

Still other studies suggest that some forms of serious crime—forms usually associated with lower-class youth— show up *more frequently* among higher-class persons than among lower.[13] For instance, Empey and Erikson interviewed 180 white males aged 15 to 17 who were drawn from different economic strata. They found that "virtually all respondents reported having committed not one but a variety of different offenses." Although youngsters from the middle classes constituted 55 percent of the group interviewed, they owned up to 67 percent of the instances of breaking and entering, 70 percent of the instances of property destruction, and an astounding 87 percent of all the armed robberies admitted to by the entire sample.[14] Williams and Gold studied a national sample of 847 males and females between the ages of 13 and 16.[15] Of these, 88 percent admitted to at least one delinquent offense. Eugene Doleschal writes of the Williams-Gold study,

> In support of recent studies, this research found that the relationship between social status and delinquent behavior was weak except that *higher-status white boys were more delinquent than lower-status white boys.* The greater seriousness

of the higher-status boys' delinquent behavior stemmed from their committing proportionally more thefts, joy riding, and (surprisingly) assaults.[16]

Even those who conclude "that more lower status youngsters commit delinquent acts more frequently than do higher status youngsters"[17] recognize that lower-class youth are significantly overrepresented in official records. Gold writes that "about five times more lowest than highest status boys appear in the official records; if records were complete and unselective, we estimate that the ratio would be closer to 1.5:1."[18] The simple fact is that for the same offense, *a poor person is more likely to be arrested, and if arrested charged, than a middle- or upper-class person.*[19]

This means, first of all, that poor people are more likely to come to the attention of the police. Furthermore, even when apprehended, the police are more likely to formally charge a poor person and release a higher-class person *for the same offense.* Gold writes that

> boys who live in poorer parts of town and are apprehended by police for delinquency are four to five times more likely to appear in some official record than boys from wealthier sections who commit *the same kinds of offenses.* These same data show that, at each stage in the legal process from charging a boy with an offense to some sort of disposition in court, boys from different socio-economic backgrounds are treated differently, so that those eventually incarcerated in public institutions, that site of most of the research on delinquency, are *selectively poorer boys.*[20]

Based on a study of self-reported delinquent behavior, Gold finds than when individuals were apprehended, "if the offender came from a higher status family, police were more likely to handle the matter themselves without referring it to the court."[21]

Terence Thornberry reaches a similar conclusion in a more recent study of 3475 delinquent boys in Philadelphia. Thornberry found that among boys arrested *for equally serious offenses* and who had *similar prior offense records*, police were more likely to refer the lower-class youths than the more affluent ones to juvenile court. The police were more likely to deal with the wealthier youngsters informally, for example, by holding them in the station house until their parents came rather than instituting formal procedures. Of those referred to juvenile court, Thornberry found further that for *equally serious offenses* and with *similar prior records*, the poorer youngsters were more likely to be institutionalized than were the affluent ones. The wealthier youths were more likely to receive probation that the poorer ones. As might be expected, Thornberry found the same relationships when comparing the treatment of black and white youths apprehended for equally serious offenses.[22]

Ronald Goldfarb cites a 1966 study in Contra Costa County, California, performed under the auspices of the President's Committee on Juvenile Delinquency and Youth Development, which further supports these conclusions:

> 48.2 percent of juveniles arrested in California were released by the police after some informal handling and without charges being preferred. But in the upper-middle-class suburban community of Lafayette in Contra Costa County, 80 percent were released after arrests. Of the total juveniles arrested in California, 46.5 percent were referred to a juvenile court; in Layfayette, 17.9 percent. Of those who eventually were institutionalized, the California average was 5.3 percent; in Lafayette County, 1.3 percent.[23]

Lest you conclude that these differences are only true of young offenders, it would be wise to keep in mind that this group accounts for much of the "crime problem"—43 percent of total police arrests in the United States in 1974 were of persons under 21 years old[24]—and many commentators have blamed this group above others for the rapid increase in crime in recent years. Beyond this, other studies, not limited to the young, bear out the same economic bias.

For example, a study of drunken driving "demonstrated that minority group members, the lower class, males, and youth are consistently more likely to be convicted of driving while intoxicated than are whites, the upper class, and older persons."[25] A study of the treatment of employee theft found that *for the same amount stolen* "more lower status employees (cleaners, servicemen, stock personnel) than higher status ones (executives, salespersons, white collar workers) were prosecuted. A significantly larger proportion of the former (73 percent) than of the latter (50 percent) were prosecuted."[26]

Any number of reasons can be offered to account for these differences in treatment. Some argue that they reflect the fact that the poor have less privacy.[27] What others can do in their living rooms or backyards, the poor do on the street. Others argue that a police officer's decision to book a poor youth and release a middle-class youth reflects either the officer's judgment that the higher-class youngster's family will be more likely and more able to discipline him or her than the lower-class youngster's or differences in the degree to which poor and middle-class complainants demand arrest. Others argue that police training and police work condition police officers to be suspicious of certain kinds of people, such as lower-class youth, blacks, Mexicans, and so on,[28] and thus more likely to detect their criminality. Still others hold that police mainly arrest those with the least political clout,[29] those who are least able to focus public attention on police practices or bring political influence to bear, and these happen to be the members of the lowest social and economic classes.

Regardless of which view one takes, and probably all have some truth in them, one conclusion is inescapable: one of the reasons that the offender "at the end of the road in prison is likely to be a member of the lowest social and economic groups in the country" is that the police officers who guard the access to the road to prison make sure that more poor people will make the trip than well-to-do people.

The *weeding out of the wealthy* starts at the very entrance to the criminal justice system: the decision about whom to investigate, arrest, or charge is not made simply on the basis of the offense committed or the danger posed. It is a decision that is distorted by a systematic economic bias that works to the disadvantage of the poor.

This economic bias is a two-edged sword. Not only are the poor arrested and charged out of proportion to their numbers for the kinds of crimes poor people generally commit—burglary, robbery, assault and so forth—but when we reach the kinds of crimes poor people almost never have the opportunity to commit—antitrust violations, industrial safety violations, embezzlement, serious tax evasion—the criminal justice system shows an increasingly benign and merciful face: the more likely it is that a crime is the type committed by middle- and upper-class folks, the less likely that it will be treated as a criminal offense. When it comes to crime in the streets, where the perpetrator is apt to be poor, he or she is even more likely to be arrested, formally charged, and so on. When it comes to crime in the suites, where the offender is apt to be affluent, the system is most likely to deal with the crime noncriminally, that is, by civil litigation or informal settlement. Where it does choose to proceed criminally, as we shall see in the section on sentencing, it rarely goes beyond a slap on the wrist. Not only is the main entry to the road to prison held wide open to the poor, but the access routes for the wealthy are largely sealed off. Once again, we should not be surprised at who we find in our prisons.

Many writers have commented on the extent and seriousness of "white-collar crime," so I will keep my remarks to a minimum. Nevertheless, for those of us trying to understand how the image of crime is created, four points should be noted.

1. White-collar crime is costly; it takes far more dollars from our pockets than all the FBI Index Crimes combined.
2. White-collar crime is widespread, probably much more so than the colored-collar variety.
3. White-collar criminals are rarely arrested or charged; the system has developed kindlier ways of dealing with the more delicate sensibilities of its higher-class clientele.

4. When white-collar criminals are prosecuted and con-
    victed, their sentences are either suspended or very light
    when judged by the cost their crimes have imposed
    on society.

The first three points will be discussed here, and the fourth
will be presented in the section on sentencing below.

The U.S. Chamber of Commerce estimates conservatively
(as it does most everything else) that white-collar crimes cost
over $40 billion annually![30] (See Table 3.) This is over *250
times* the amount taken in all the bank robberies in the
United States in 1974.[31] It is more than *ten times* the total
amount taken in all the thefts reported in the FBI Index for
that year.[32] A decade ago, the President's Crime Commission
reported that

> estimates of the amount of reportable income that goes
> unreported each year range from $25 to $40 billion. Some of
> this is inadvertent, but undoubtedly a sizeable amount is
> deliberate, criminal evasion. The financial loss to the public
> caused by a single conspiracy in restraint of trade may be
> untold millions in extra costs paid ultimately by the buying
> public. It is estimated that the cost to the public annually of
> securities frauds, while impossible to quantify with any cer-
> tainty, is probably in the $500 million to $1 billion range. A
> conservative estimate is that nearly $500 million is spent
> annually on worthless or extravagantly misrepresented drugs
> and therapeutic devices. Fraudulent and deceptive practices in
> the home repair and improvement field are said to result in
> $500 million to $1 billion losses annually; and in the auto-
> mobile repair field alone, fraudulent practices have been
> estimated to cost $100 million annually.[33]

Another observer claims that unreported taxable income
may cost "the national treasury $4 to $5 billion annually."[34]
In any event, it should be kept in mind that all of these
actions are just as much theft as the most commonly
recognized forms. If taxable income goes unreported, others
must pay more taxes to make up the difference. If corporations engage in price-fixing, then consumers must pay

Table 3   The Cost of White-Collar Crime

(Billions of Dollars)		
Bankruptcy fraud		$ 0.08
Bribery, kickbacks, and payoffs		3.00
Computer-related crime		0.10
Consumer fraud, illegal competition, Deceptive practices		21.00
Consumer victims:	$ 5.5	
Business victims:	$ 3.5	
Government revenue loss:	$12.0	
Credit card and check fraud		1.10
Credit card:	$ 0.1	
Check:	$ 1.0	
Embezzlement and pilferage		7.0
Embezzlement (cash, goods, services):	$ 3.0	
Pilferage:	$ 4.0	
Insurance Fraud		2.00
Insurer victims:	$ 1.5	
Policyholder victims:	$ 0.5	
Receiving stolen property		3.50
Securities thefts and frauds		4.00
	Total (billions)	$41.78

Source: Chamber of Commerce of the United States, *A Handbook on White-Collar Crime*, 1974.

higher prices than they would under free competiton. If businesses lose money to embezzlers, they pass the costs (including the costs of higher insurance premiums) on to the consumer in the form of higher prices. In all these cases, individuals may not "feel" victimized, but the impact on them is in every other respect the same as if they had been held up at gunpoint: they have fewer dollars in their pockets than they would otherwise have.

In addition to fraud and tax evasion by individuals, corporate crime is also rampant. Sutherland, in a study that has become a classic in its field, analyzed the "behavior" of 70 of the largest U.S. corporations over a period of some 40 years:

> The records reveal that every one of the seventy corporations had violated one or more of the laws, with an average of about thirteen adverse decisions per corporation and a range of from one to fifty adverse decisions per corporation. The corporations had a total of 307 adverse decisions on charges of restraint of trade, 222 adverse decisions on charges of infringements [of patents, trademarks, and copyrights], 158 adverse decisions under the National Labor Relations Act, 97 adverse decisions under the laws regulating advertising, and 196 adverse decisions on charges of violating other laws. Thus, generally, the official records reveal that these corporations violated the trade regulations with great frequency. The "habitual criminal" laws of some states impose severe penalties on criminals convicted the third or fourth time. If this criterion were used here, about *90 percent of the large corporations studied would be considered habitual white-collar criminals.*[35]

Nevertheless, corporate executives almost never end up in jail, where they would find themselves sharing cells with poorer persons who had stolen less from their fellow citizens.

There are many reasons for this. Perhaps most important is the fact that with many of these law violations, the government has the choice to proceed criminally *or* civilly and usually chooses the latter. That is, with upper-class lawbreakers, the authorities prefer to sue in civil court for damages or for an injunction rather than treat the wealthy as common criminals. Judges have on occasion stated in open court that they "would not make criminals of reputable businessmen."[36] One would think that it would be up to the businessmen to make criminals of themselves by their actions, but alas, *this* right is reserved for the lower classes.

Another tool that the government uses to spare the corporate executive the trials of criminality, is the consent decree. Senator Philip Hart said of the consent decree that it "is a negotiated instrument whereby a firm, in effect, says it has done nothing wrong and promises never to do it again.

The agreement is filed in court and that's the end of it, unless the firm is caught doing it again."[37] Imagine if this were available to burglars. Instead of arresting them and giving them a criminal record, the police would ask them to sign a statement promising never to do it again and file it in court, but alas, *this* alternative is reserved for a higher class of thief.

Examples of reluctance to use the full force of the criminal process for crimes not generally committed by the poor can be multiplied ad nauseam. Let me close with one final example that typifies this particular distortion of criminal justice policy.

Embezzlement is the crime of misappropriating money or property entrusted to one's care, custody, or control. Since the poor are rarely entrusted with tempting sums of money or valuable property, this is predominantly a crime of the middle and upper classes. The U.S. Chamber of Commerce estimates the annual economic cost of embezzlement at *three billion dollars*,[38] roughly equivalent to the total value of the money and property stolen in all FBI Index Property Crimes in 1974. Thus, it is fair to conclude that embezzlement poses about the same cost to society as do FBI Index Property Crimes. Nevertheless, the FBI reports that in 1974, when there were 1,731,000 arrests for burglary, larceny, and motor vehicle theft, there were 13,000 arrests for embezzlement nationwide. Although burglary, larceny, and motor vehicle theft cost the nation about the same as embezzlement, the number of arrests for them was *133 times greater* than the number of arrests for embezzlement.[39] Using very rough figures, this means there was more than one arrest for a property crime for every $2000 stolen and less than one arrest for embezzlement for every $200,000 "misappropriated." Note that even the language becomes more delicate as we deal with a better class of crook.

The clientele of the criminal justice system form an exclusive club. Entry is largely a privilege of the poor. The crimes they commit are the crimes that qualify one for admission—and they are admitted in greater proportion than their share of those crimes. Curiously enough, the crimes the affluent commit are not the kind that easily qualify one for membership in the club.

2. Convictions

Between arrest and imprisonment lies the crucial process that determines guilt or innocence. Studies of individuals accused of similar offenses and with similar prior records show that the poor defendant is more likely to be adjudicated guilty than is the wealthier defendant.[40] In the adjudication process the only thing that *should* count is whether the accused is guilty and whether the prosecution can prove it beyond a reasonable doubt. Unfortunately, at least two other factors that are irrelevant to the question of guilt or innocence significantly affect the outcome: one is the ability of the accused to be free on bail prior to trial, and the second is access to legal counsel able to devote adequate time and energy to the case. Since both bail and high-quality legal counsel cost money, it should come as no surprise that here as elsewhere the poor do poorly. "A defendant in a criminal court," writes Abraham Blumberg, "is really beaten by the deprivations and limitations imposed by his social class, race and ethnicity. These in turn preclude such services as bail, legal counsel, psychiatric services, expert witnesses, and investigatory assistance. In essence the concomitants of poverty are responsible for the fact that due process sometimes produces greatly disparate results in an ill-matched struggle."[41]

Being released on bail is important in several respects. First and foremost, of course, is the fact that those who are not released on bail are kept in jail like individuals who have been found guilty. They are thus punished while they are still legally innocent. In 1972, 51,000 (out of a total of 142,000) inmates of local jails were confined while awaiting trial. Their average pretrial or presentence confinement was three months, and 60 percent of the nation's jails do not separate pretrial defendants from convicted offenders. Beyond the obvious ugliness of punishing people before they are found guilty, confined defendants suffer from other disabilities. Specifically, they cannot actively aid in their own defense by seeking out witnesses and evidence. Several studies have shown that among defendants accused of the same offenses, those who make bail are more likely to be acquitted than those who do not.[42]

Furthermore, since the time spent in jail prior to adjudication of guilt may count as part of the sentence if one is found guilty, the accused are often placed in a ticklish position. Let us say the accused believes that he or she is innocent or at least that the state cannot prove guilt, and let us say also that her or she has been in the slammer for two months awaiting trial. Along comes the prosecutor to offer a deal: If you plead guilty to such-and-such (usually a lesser offense than has been charged, e.g., possession of burglar's tools instead of burglary), the prosecutor promises to ask the judge to sentence you to two months. In other words, plead guilty and walk out of jail today—or maintain your innocence, stay in jail until trial, and then be tried for the full charge instead of the lesser offense! Plea-bargaining is an everyday occurrence in the criminal justice system. Contrary to the Perry Mason image, the vast majority of criminal convictions in the United States are reached without a trial. It is estimated that between 70 and 95 percent of convictions are the result of a negotiated plea,[43] that is, a bargain in which the accused agrees to plead guilty (usually to a lesser offense than he or she is charged with or to one offense out of many he or she is charged with) in return for an informal promise of leniency from the prosecutor with the tacit consent of the judge. If you were the jailed defendant offered a deal like this, how would you choose? Suppose you were a poor black man not likely to be able to retain F. Lee Bailey or Edward Bennett Williams for your defense?

The advantages of access to adequate legal counsel during the adjudicative process are obvious but still worthy of mention. In 1963, the U.S. Supreme Court handed down the landmark *Gideon* v. *Wainwright* decision, holding that the states must provide legal counsel to the indigent in all felony cases. As a result, no person accused of a serious crime need

face their accusers without a lawyer. However, the Supreme
Court has not held that the Constitution requires that
individuals are entitled to lawyers able to devote equal time
and resources to their cases. Even though *Gideon* represents
significant progress in making good on the Constitutional
promise of equal treatment before the law, we still are left
with two transmission belts of justice: one for the poor and
one for the affluent. There is, to be sure, an emerging body of
case law on the right to effective assistance of counsel;[44]
however, this is yet to have any serious impact on the
assembly-line legal aid handed out to the poor.

Indigent defendants, those who cannot afford to retain
their own lawyers, will be defended either by a public
defender or by a private attorney assigned by the court. Since
the public defender is a salaried attorney with a case load
much larger than that of a private criminal lawyer,[45] and
since court-assigned private attorneys are paid a fixed fee
that is much lower than they charge their regular clients,
neither is able or motivated to devote much time to the
indigent defendant's defense. Both are strongly motivated to
bring their cases to a close quickly by negotiating a plea of
guilty. Since the public defender works in day-to-day contact
with the prosecutor and the judge, the pressures on him or
her to negotiate a plea as quickly as possible, instead of
rocking the boat by threatening to go to trial,[46] are even
greater than those that work on court-assigned counsel. In
an essay, aptly entitled "Did You Have a Lawyer When You
Went to Court? No, I Had a Public Defender," Jonathan
Casper reports the perceptions of this process from the
standpoint of the defendants:

> Most of the men spent very little time with their public
> defender. In the court in which they eventually plead guilty,
> they typically reported spending on the order of five to ten
> minutes with their public defender. These conversations usu-
> ally took place in the bull-pen of the courthouse or in the
> hallway.
> The brief conversations usually did not involve much dis-
> cussion of the details surrounding the alleged crime, mitigat-

ing circumstances or the defendant's motives or backgrounds. Instead, they focused on the deal, the offer the prosecution was likely to make or had made in return for a cop out. Often the defendants reported that the first words the public defender spoke (or at least the first words the defendants recalled) were, "I can get you . . . , if you plead guilty."[47]

Abraham S. Blumberg studied 724 male felony defendants who pleaded guilty in a large metropolitan court. He found that in the majority of cases it was the defense counsel who first suggested a guilty plea and who most influenced the defendant's decision to plead guilty. More striking still, however, was the finding that public defenders and court-assigned lawyers suggested the plea of guilty *earlier* than privately retained attorneys. On this, Blumberg comments, "Legal-aid and assigned counsel are apparently more likely to suggest the plea in the initial interview, perhaps as a response to pressures of time and, in the case of the assigned counsel, the strong possibility that there is no fee involved."[48] Privately retained counsel suggested the plea in the initial meeting in 35 percent of their cases, public defenders in 49 percent, and assigned counsel in 60 percent.[49] It should be noted that Blumberg concludes that these differences have little impact on the eventual outcome. Other findings point to a different conclusion.

As might be expected, with less time and resources to devote to the cause, public defenders and assigned lawyers cannot devote as much time and research to preparing the crucial pretrial motions that can often lead to dismissal of charges against the accused. One study shows that public defenders got dismissals in 8 percent of their cases, assigned lawyers in 6 percent, and privately retained counsel in *29 percent of their cases.*[50] And, as also might be expected, the overall aquittal rate for privately retained counsel is considerably better than that for public defenders and assigned counsel. The same study shows that public defenders achieved either dismissal of charges or a finding of not guilty in 17 percent of the indictments they handled, assigned counsel did the same in 18 percent, and privately retained counsel got their clients off the hook in *36 percent of their indictments*. The picture that emerges from the federal courts is not much different.[51]

Needless to say, the distinct legal advantages that money can buy become even more salient when we enter the realm of corporate and other white-collar crime. Indeed, it is often precisely the time and cost involved in bringing to court a large corporation with its army of legal eagles that is offered as an excuse for the less formal and more genteel treatment accorded to corporate crooks. This excuse is, of course, not equitably distributed to all economic classes, anymore than quality legal service is. What this means in simple terms is that regardless of actual innocence or guilt, one's chances of beating the rap increase as one's income increases. Regardless of what fraction of crimes are committed by the poor, the criminal justice system is distorted so that an even greater fraction of those convicted will be poor. And with conviction comes sentencing.

3. Sentencing

He had a businessman's suit and a businessman's tan, but Jack L. Clark no longer had a business. His nursing home construction company had collapsed in a gigantic stock fraud, leaving shareholders out $200 million and leaving Clark in a federal courthouse, awaiting sentence for stock manipulation. Ten million of the swindled dollars had allegedly gone for Clark's personal use, and prosecutors accused him of stashing away 4 million unrecovered dollars in a retirement nest egg. Out of an original indictment of 65 counts, Clark had pleaded guilty to one charge. He faced a maximum penalty of a $10,000 fine and five years in prison. But the judge, before passing sentence, remembered the "marked improvement" in care for the elderly that Clark's nursing homes had provided . . . He considered that Clark was a 46-year-old family man who coached little kids in baseball and football. Then he passed sentence. No fine. One year in prison. Eligible for parole after four months.

In another federal courtroom stood Matthew Corelli (not his real name), a 45-year-old, $125-a-week laborer who lived with his wife and kids in a $126-a-month apartment. Along with three other men, Corelli had been convicted of possessing $5,000 of stolen drugstore goods that government prosecutors identified as part of a $63,000 shipment. The judge considered Corelli's impoverished circumstances, his number of dependents, the nature of his crime, and then passed sentence: four years in prison. Or in other words, four times the punishment Clark received for a fraction of the crime.[52]

Jack Greenberg took $15 from a post office; last May in Federal Court in Manhattan he drew six months in jail. Howard Lazell "misapplied" $150,000 from a bank; in the same month in the same courthouse he drew probation.[53]

The first quotation is the opening passage of a magazine article on white-collar crime, aptly titled "America's Most Coddled Criminals." The second quotation is the opening paragraph of a *New York Times* article, more prosaically titled "Wide Disparities Mark Sentences Here." Both, however, are testimony to the fact that the criminal justice system reserves it harshest penalties for its lower-class clients and puts on kid gloves when confronted with a better class of crook.

The system is doubly biased against the poor. First, there is the class bias *between* crimes that we have just seen. The crimes that poor people are likely to commit carry harsher sentences than the "crimes in the suites" committed by well-to-do people. Second, for *all* crimes, the poor receive less probation and more years of confinement than better-heeled defendants *convicted of the same offense,* assuring us once again that the vast majority of those who are put behind bars are from the lowest social and economic classes in the nation.

The *New York Times* article referred to above reported the results of a study done by the *New York Times* on sentencing in state and federal courts. The *Times* reports that "crimes that tend to be committed by the poor get tougher sentences than those committed by the well-to-do," that federal "defendants who could not afford private counsel were sentenced nearly twice as severely as defendants with private or no counsel," and that a "study by the Vera Institute of Justice of courts in the Bronx indicates a similar pattern in the state courts."[54]

Looking at federal and state courts, Stuart Nagel concludes that

> not only are the indigent found guilty more often, but they are much less likely to be recommended for probation by the probation officer, or to be granted probation or suspended sentences by the judge.

And, further, that

> the federal data show that this is true also of those with *no* prior record: 27 percent of the indigent with no prior record were *not* recommended for probation against 16 percent of the non-indigent; 23 percent indigent did *not* receive suspended sentences or probation against 15 percent non-indigent. Among those of both groups with "some" prior record the spread is even greater.[55]

Eugene Doleschal and Nora Klapmuts report as "typical of American studies," Thornberry's analysis of "3,475 Philadelphia delinquents that found that blacks and members of lower socioeconomic groups were likely to receive more severe dispositions than whites and the more affluent even when the appropriate legal variables [i.e., offense, prior record, etc.] were held constant."[56]

As usual, data on racial discrimination in sentencing exist in much greater abundance than data on class discrimination, but they tell the same story of the treatment of those who cannot afford the going price of justice. Most striking perhaps is the fact that over 40 percent of the inmates of all correctional facilities in the United States—state and federal prisons as well as local jails—are black, while blacks account for a little over one-quarter of all arrests in the nation. Even when we compare the percentage of blacks arrested for serious (i.e., FBI Index) crimes with the percentage of blacks in federal and state prisons (where presumably those convicted of such offenses would be sent), blacks still make up over 40 percent of the inmates but only about 36 percent of the

arrestees, which is still a considerable disparity. Furthermore, when we look at federal prisons, where there is reason
to believe racial and economic discrimination is less prevalent than in state institutions, we find that the average sentence for a white inmate in 1972 was 45.4 months, as compared to 59.1 months (over a year more!) for nonwhite inmates.
The nonwhite inmate serves, on the average, 3 more months
than a white inmate for burglary, 21 more months for a drug
law violation, and more than twice as long for income tax
evasion![57]

Studies have confirmed that black burglars receive longer
sentences than do white burglars. And blacks who plead
guilty receive harsher sentences than whites who do, although by an act of dubious mercy of which Americans
ought hardly be proud, blacks often receive lighter sentences
for murder and rape than whites as long as the victim was
black as well.[58] Mary Owen Cameron studied the sentencing
practices of judges in the Chicago Women's Court during a
three-year period. Her findings were as follows:

> Judges found sixteen percent of the white women brought
> before them on charges of shoplifting to be "not guilty," but
> only four percent of the black women were found innocent. In
> addition, twenty-two percent of the black women as compared
> to four percent of the white women were sent to jail. Finally, of
> the twenty-one white women sentenced to jail, only two (ten
> percent) were to be jailed for thirty days or more; of the
> seventy-six black women sentenced to jail, twenty (twenty-six
> percent) were to be jailed for thirty days or more.[59]

Many studies have shown that blacks convicted of murder
or of rape—where rape is a capital offense—are much more
likely to be sentenced to death than are whites, except where
the victim is black.[60] Another study has shown that among
blacks and whites on death row, whites are more likely to
have their sentences commuted. And blacks or whites who
have private counsel are more likely to have their execution
commuted than condemned persons defended by court-
appointed attorneys.[61]

As I have already pointed out, justice is increasingly tempered with mercy as we deal with a better class of crime. The Sherman Antitrust Act is a criminal law. It was passed in recognition of the fact that one virtue of a free enterprise economy is that competition tends to drive consumer prices down, so agreements by competing firms to refrain from price competition is the equivalent of stealing money from the consumer's pocket. Nevertheless, although such conspiracies cost consumers far more than lower-class theft, price-fixing was a misdemeanor until 1974.[62] In practice, few conspirators end up in prison, and when they do, the sentence is a mere token, well below the maximum provided in the law. Thus, based on the government's track record, there is little reason to expect things to change significantly now that price-fixing is a felony.

In the historic *Electrical Equipment* cases in the early 1960s, executives of several major firms secretly met to fix prices on electrical equipment to a degree that is estimated to have cost the buying public well over a billion dollars. The executives involved knew they were violating the law. They used plain envelopes for their communications, called their meetings "choir practice," and referred to the list of executives in attendance as the "Christmas card list." This case is rare and famous because it was one in which the criminal sanction was actually imposed. Seven executives received and served jail sentences. But in light of the amount of money they had stolen from the American public, their sentences were more an indictment of the government than of themselves: *30 days in jail!*

The President's Crime Commission reports "that since that case no antitrust defendant has been imprisoned. In seven cases since then, involving 45 individual defendants, prison sentences were imposed, but in each case the sentence was suspended." In any event, the commission reports that "the Antitrust Division does not feel that lengthy prison sentences are ordinarily called for. It 'rarely recommends jail sentences greater than 6 months—recommendations of 30-day imprisonment are most frequent.'"[63]

In general the crimes of the poor receive stiffer sentences than the crimes of the well-to-do. For instance, Marvin Frankel points out, in his book *Criminal Sentences: Law Without Order*, that "of 502 defendants convicted for income tax fraud 95, or 19 percent, received prison terms, the average being three months. Of 3,791 defendants sentenced for auto theft, 2,373, or 63 percent, went to prison, the average term being 7.6 months."[64] More recent figures fit this pattern. A statistical report of the Federal Bureau of Prisons yields information about the average sentences received by inmates of federal institutions and the average time served until parole (see Table 4).

Table 4   Sentences for Different Classes of Crime

	Average Sentence (in months)	Average Time Until Parole (in months)
Crimes of the poor		
Robbery	133.3	51.2
Burglary	58.7	30.2
Larceny/theft	32.8	18.7
Crimes of the affluent		
Embezzlement	21.1	13.2
Fraud	27.2	14.3
Income tax evasion	12.8	9.7

Source. Federal Bureau of Prisons—Statistical Report, Fiscal Year 1973.

Keep in mind while looking at these figures that *each* of the "crimes of the affluent" costs the public more than *all* of the "crimes of the poor" put together.

A study of sentencing practices in the Southern District of New York, optimistically entitled *Justice in Sentencing*, found

plain indications that white collar defendants, predominantly white, receive more lenient treatment as a general rule, while defendants charged with common crimes, largely committed by the unemployed and undereducated, a group which embraces large numbers of blacks in today's society, are more likely to be sent to prison. If these indications are correct, then one may conclude that poor persons receive harsher treatment in the Federal Courts than do well-to-do defendants charged with more sophisticated crimes.

Specifically, the study reports that "during the six-month period covered by the Southern District of New York sentencing study, *defendants convicted of white collar crimes stood a 36% chance of going to prison; defendants convicted of nonviolent common crimes stood a 53% chance of going to prison*; and defendants convicted of violent crimes stood an 80% chance of going to prison."[65] Several things are worthy of note here. First, the study carries forth the distorted conventional wisdom about crime by distinguishing between "white-collar" and "common" crime, when, as we have found, there is every reason to believe that white-collar crime is just as common as the so-called common crimes of the poor. Second, the disparities reported refer only to likelihood of imprisonment *for any length of time*, and so they really understate the disparities in treatment, since the so-called common crimes also receive *longer* prison sentences than the white-collar crimes. But third, and most importantly, the disparities cannot be explained by the greater danger of lower-class criminals because even the perpetrators of *nonviolent common crimes* stand a 50 percent greater chance of going to prison than do white-collar crooks.

A graphic illustration of the way the criminal justice system treats the wealthy is provided by Fleetwood and Lubow in their article "America's Most Coddled Criminals." They put together their pick of ten convicted white-collar criminals, comparing their sentences with the crimes they committed. The chart speaks for itself (see Table 5).

Equally eloquent testimony to the merciful face that the criminal justice system turns toward upper-class crooks is to be found in a *New York Times* report on the fate of 21 business executives found guilty of making illegal campaign contributions during the Watergate scandal:

Table 5 Ten Bandits: What They Did and What They Got

This isn't the Chamber of Commerce list of brightest young businessmen, and it's not the ten best-dressed list. It's a list of ten very respectable criminals. Have any favorites you don't see here? Send them in.

Criminal	Crime	Sentence
Jack L. Clark	President and chairman of Four Seasons Nursing Centers, Clark finagled financial reports and earnings projections to inflate his stock artificially. Shareholders lost $200 million.	One year in prison.
John Peter Galanis	As portfolio manager of two mutual funds, Galanis bilked investors out of nearly $10 million.	Six months in prison and five years probation.
Virgil A. McGowen	As manager of the Bank of America branch in San Francisco, McGowen siphoned off $591,921 in clandestine loans to friends. Almost none of the money was recovered.	Six months in prison, five years probation and a $3,600 fine.
Valdemar H. Madis	A wealthy drug manufacturer, Madis diluted an antidote for poisoned children with a worthless, look-alike substance.	One year probation and a $10,000 fine.
John Morgan	President of Jet Craft Ltd, John Morgan illegally sold about $2 million in unregistered securities.	One year in prison and a $10,000 fine.
Irving Projansky	The former chairman of the First National Bank of Lincolnwood, Ill., Projansky raised stock prices artificially and then dumped the shares, costing the public and estimated $4 million.	One year in prison and two years probation.

Table 5 Ten Bandits: What They Did and What They Got (cont'd)

David Ratliff	Ratliff spent his 21 years as a Texas state senator embezzling state funds.	Ten years probation.
Walter J. Rauscher	An executive vice-president of American Airlines, Rauscher accepted about $200,000 in kickbacks from businessmen bidding for contracts.	Six months in prison and two years probation.
Frank W. Sharp	The multimillion-dollar swindles of Sharp, a Houston banker, shook the Texas state government and forced the resignation of the head of the Criminal Division of the Justice Dept.	Three years probation and a $5,000 fine.
Seymour R. Thaler	Soon after his election to the New York State Supreme Court, Thaler was convicted of receiving and transporting $800,000 in stolen U.S. Treasury bills.	One year in prison and a fine of $10,000.

Source. Blake Fleetwood and Arthur Lubow, "America's Most Coddled Crimnals," *New Times Magazine,* September 19, 1975.

Most of the 21 business executives who admitted their guilt to
the Watergate Special Prosecutor in 1973 and 1974—especially
those from large corporations—are still presiding over their
companies. . . .
   Only two went to jail. They served a few months and were
freed. . . .
   Furthermore, the fines of $1,000 or $2,000 that most of the
contributors of illegal funds had to pay have not made much of
a dent in their style of living. . . .
   An investigation into the whereabouts and financial status
of the 21 executives involved in illegal contributions leads to a
conclusion that the higher the position the more cushioned the
fall—if indeed there was a fall.[66]

The *Times* report also includes a chart illustrating the fate of
these upper-class criminals, who were found guilty of nothing less than participating in schemes that undermine the
independence of the electoral process—guilty, that is, of
contaminating the very lifeblood of democratic government.
Here, again, the chart speaks for itself (see Table 6).
   On either side of the law, the rich get richer...

b.   ... And the Poor Get Prison

At 9:05 A.M. on the morning of Thursday, September 9, 1971, a
group of inmates forced their way through a gate at the
center of the prison, fatally injured a guard named William
Quinn, and took 50 hostages. The Attica uprising had begun.
It lasted almost exactly four days, until 9:43 A.M. on the
morning of Monday, September 13, when corrections officers
and state troopers stormed the prison and killed 10 hostages
and 29 inmates.[67] During those four days the nation saw on
its TV sets the faces of its captives. They were the hard black
faces of young men who had grown up on the streets of
Harlem and other urban ghettos. Theirs were the faces of
crime in America. The television viewers who saw them were
not surprised. These were the faces of dangerous men who
should be locked up. Nor were people outraged when the state
launched its murderous attack on the prison, killing many

Table 6 Convicted Watergate Campaign Contributors

Company	Name	Fine/Prison	Current Status
American Ship Building	George M. Steinbrenner	$15,000	Still chairman at $50,000/year
	John H. Melcher, Jr.	$ 2,500	Discharged; practicing law in Cleveland
Ashland Oil	Orin E. Atkins[a]	$ 1,000	Still chairman at $314,000/year
Associated Milk Producers	Harold S. Nelson	4 months prison $10,000	Resigned; now in commodities exports
	David L. Parr	4 months prison $10,000	Resigned
	Stuart H. Russell	2 years prison[b]	Resigned; now in private law practice
Braniff International	Harding L. Lawrence	$ 1,000	Still chairman at $335,000/year
Carnation	H. Everett Olson	$ 1,000	Still chairman at $212,500/year
Diamond International	Ray Dubrowin	$ 1,000	Still V.P. for public affairs
Goodyear Tire and Rubber	Russell DeYoung	$ 1,000	Still chairman of 2 committees at $306,000/year and pension $144,000/year
Gulf Oil	Claude C. Wild, Jr.	$ 1,000	Consultant in Washington, D.C.
HMS Electric	Charles H. Huseman	$ 1,000	Still president
LBC&W Inc.	Willian G. Lyles, Sr.	$ 2,000	Still chairman

Table 6 Convicted Watergate Campaign Contributors (cont'd)

Lehigh Valley Cooperative Farmers	Richard L. Allison	$ 1,000 (suspended)	Discharged
3M	Harry Heltzer	$ 500	Retired as chairman, does special projects at $100,000/year
Northrop	Thomas V. Jones	$ 5,000	Still chief executive at $286,000/year
	James Allen	$ 1,000	Retired as V.P. with pension est. at $36,000/year
Phillips Petroleum	William W. Keeler	$ 1,000	Retired, with pension est. at $201,742/year
Ratrie, Robbins and Schweitzer	Harry Ratrie	1 month probation	Still president
	Augustus Robbins III	1 month probation	Still executive V.P.
Time Oil	Raymond Abendroth	$ 2,000	Still president

Source. Michael C. Jensen, "Watergate Donors Still Riding High," *The New York Times*, August 24, 1975
[a] Pleaded no contest. [b] Under appeal.

more prisoners and guards than did the rioters themselves. Maybe they were shocked—but not outraged. Nor were they outraged when two grand juries refused to indict any of the attackers, nor when the mastermind of the attack, then-Governor Nelson Rockefeller, was named to be vice-President of the United States three years after the uprising and massacre.[68]

They were not outraged, because the faces they saw on the TV screens fit and confirmed their beliefs about who is a deadly threat to American society—and a deadly threat must be met with deadly force. But how did those men get to Attica? And how did Americans get their beliefs about who is a dangerous person? Obviously, these questions are interwoven. People get their notions about who is a criminal at least in part from the occasional TV or newspaper picture of who is inside our prisons. And the individuals they see there have been put there because people believe that certain kinds of individuals are dangerous and should be locked up.

I have tried to argue in this chapter that this is not a simple process of selecting the dangerous and the criminal from among the peace-loving and the law-abiding. It is also a process of *weeding out the wealthy* at every stage, so that the final picture—a picture like that which appeared on the TV screen on September 9, 1971—is not a true reflection of the real dangers in our society but a distorted image, the kind reflected in a carnival mirror.

It is not my view that the inmates in Attica were innocent of the crimes that sent them there. I am willing to assume that they and just about all the individuals in prisons in America are probably guilty of the crime for which they were sentenced and maybe more. My point is that people who are equally or more dangerous, equally or more criminal, are not there; that the criminal justice system works systematically, not to punish and confine the dangerous and the criminal, *but to punish and confine the* **poor** *who are dangerous and criminal.*

And it is successful at all levels. Of the 7724 inmates of *federal* prisons and reformatories in 1970 who had an income in 1969, 4491 (nearly 60 percent) reported an annual income of under $2000.[69] Of 141,600 persons confined in *local* jails throughout the nation in mid-1972, 61,800 (44 percent) had a prearrest annual income of less than $2000—only 11 percent reported a prearrest income of $7500 or more. "The 1972 U.S. median income of $9255 was exceeded by roughly 10 percent of the inmates. Only 6 percent had prearrest incomes of more than $10,000"[70] The U.S. Bureau of the Census conducted a nationwide survey of inmates of *state* correctional facilities for the Law Enforcement Assistance Administration in January 1974. They found 191,400 persons confined in state institutions; of these, 98 percent (187,500) were serving sentences—the remainder was made up of persons awaiting trial or drug addicts who "voluntarily" had submitted to treatment in lieu of being sentenced and so on. Sixty-one percent of the sentenced inmates had less than a high school education, as compared with 48 percent of the males age 18 and over in the general population. Of 168,300 state inmates who had held a full-time job after December 1968 or who had been employed during most of the month prior to their arrest, 40,000 (24 percent) reported income of less than $2000 for the year prior to arrest. Sixty percent reported income of under $6000 for the year prior to arrest. The median annual prearrest income of these 168,300 state inmates was $4639. About 69 percent of them "had worked most recently as nonfarm laborers, operatives, or craftsmen," as compared to 47 percent of employed males age 16 and over in the general population. Of the inmates who were supporting some dependents prior to arrest, 33,300 (38 percent) "reported at the time of the survey that their dependents were on welfare." And finally, of 187,500 sentenced inmates, 179,400 had been represented by legal counsel. Of these, 127,000 (more than 70 percent!) had been defended by a court-appointed lawyer or public defender or legal aid attorney. *Less than 30 percent could afford to retain their own lawyer!*[71] And so on, and on, and on.

The criminal justice system is sometimes thought of as a kind of sieve in which the innocent are progressively weeded

out from the guilty, who end up behind bars. I have tried to
show that the sieve works another way as well. It weeds the
affluent out from the poor, so it is not merely the guilty who
end up behind bars, but the *poor guilty*.

With this I think I have proven the hypotheses set forth in
Chapter 2, section c. The criminal justice system does not
simply sift the peace-loving from the dangerous, the law-
abiding from the criminal. At every stage, starting with the
very definitions of crime and progressing through the stages
of investigation, arrest, charging, conviction, and sentencing, the system *weeds out the wealthy*. It refuses to define as
"crimes" or as serious crimes the dangerous and predatory
acts of the well-to-do—acts that we have seen result in the
loss of hundreds of thousands of lives and billions of dollars.
Instead, it focuses its attention on those crimes likely to be
committed by members of the lower classes. Among those
acts defined as "crimes," the system is more likely to
investigate and detect, arrest and charge, convict and
sentence a lower-class individual than a middle- or upper-
class individual who has committed *the same offense, if not a
worse one*!

The people we see in jails and prisons may well be
dangerous to society. But they are not *the* danger to society,
not *the gravest* danger to society. Individuals who pose equal
or greater threats to our well-being walk the streets with
impunity. The criminal justice system is a mirror that hides
as much as it reveals. It is a carnival mirror that throws back
a distorted image of the dangers that lurk in our midst—and
conveys the impression that those dangers are the work of
the poor.

In Chapter 1, I argued that the criminal justice system was
rigged to fail in the fight against crime. In this chapter and in
the previous one, I have argued that the system is rigged to
make crime appear to be the monopoly of the poor. *The joint
effect of this two-way rigging is to maintain a real threat of
crime that the vast majority of Americans believes is a threat
from the poor*. In Chapter 4, I will suggest who benefits from
this illusion and how.

Footnotes

1. *Challenge*, p. 44.
2. Ronald Goldfarb, "Prisons: The National Poorhouse," *The New Republic*, November 1, 1969, pp. 15-17.
3. Philip A. Hart, "Swindling and Knavery, Inc.," *Playboy*, August 1972, p. 158.
4. Compare the statement of Professor Edwin H. Sutherland, one of the major luminaries of twentieth-century criminology: "First, the administrative processes are more favorable to persons in economic comfort than to those in poverty, so that if two persons on different economic levels are equally guilty of the same offense, the one on the lower level is more likely to be arrested, convicted, and committed to an institution. Second, the laws are written, administered and implemented primarily with reference to the types of crimes committed by people of lower economic levels." E. H. Sutherland, *Principles of Criminology* (Philadelphia: Lippincott, 1939), p. 179.
5. For example, in 1972 when blacks made up 11.3 percent of the national population, they accounted for 42.5 percent of the population of the nation's jails. *Black Population in the U.S., pp. 11, 173.*
6. Edwin H. Sutherland and Donald R. Cressey, *Criminology,* 9th edition (Philadelphia: Lippincott, 1974), p. 133. The following studies are cited (p. 133, note 4) in support of this point: Edwin M. Lemert and Judy Rosberg, "The Administration of Justice to Minority Groups in Los Angeles County," *University of California Publications in Culture and Society, 2,* No. 1 (1948), pp. 1-28; Thorsten Sellin, "Race Prejudice in the Administration of Justice," *American Journal of Sociology,* 41 (September, 1935), pp. 212-217; Sidney Alexrad, "Negro and White Male Institutionalized Delinquents," *American Journal of Sociology* 57 (May, 1952) pp. 569-574; Marvin E. Wolfgang, Arlene Kelly, and Hans C. Nolde, "Comparison of the Executed and the Commuted Among Admissions to Death Row," *Journal of Criminal Law, Criminology, and Police Science,* 53 (September, 1962), pp. 301-311; Nathan Goldman, *The Differential Selection of Juvenile Offenders for Court Appearance* (New York: National Council on Crime and Delinquency, 1963); Irving Piliavin and Scott Briar, "Police Encounters with Juveniles," *American Journal of Sociology,* 70 (Septem-

ber, 1964) pp. 206-214; Robert M. Terry, "The Screening of
Juvenile Offenders," *Journal of Criminal Law, Criminology,
and Police Science*, 58 (June, 1967), pp. 173-181. See also
Ramsey Clark, *Crime in America* (New York: Simon and
Schuster, 1970), p. 51: "Negroes are arrested more frequently
and on less evidence than whites and are more often victims
of mass or sweep arrests"; and Donald Taft, *Criminology*, 3rd
edition (New York: Macmillan, 1956), p. 134: "Negroes are
more likely to be suspected of crime than are whites. They are
also more likely to be arrested. If the perpetrator of a crime is
known to be a Negro the police may arrest all Negroes who
were near the scene—a procedure they would rarely dare to
follow with whites. After arrest Negroes are less likely to
secure bail, and so are more liable to be counted in jail statistics. They are more liable than whites to be indicted and less
likely to have their cases nol prossed or otherwise dismissed.
If tried, Negroes are more likely to be convicted. If convicted
they are less likely to be given probation. For this reason they
are more likely to be included in the count of prisoners. Negroes
are also more liable than whites to be kept in prison for the full
terms of their commitments and correspondingly less likely to
be paroled."

7. For an overview of this double distortion, see Thomas J. Dolan,
"The Case for Double Jeopardy: Black and Poor," *International Journal of Criminology and Penology*, 1 (1973),
pp. 129-150.

8. *Black Population in the U.S.*, pp. 41, 172. Furthermore, 12
percent of black jail inmates and 11 percent of the whites had
prearrest incomes of $2000 to $2999 per year, and 33 percent of
the blacks and 32 percent of the whites had prearrest incomes
of $3000 to $7499 per year. Stuart Nagel writes that "generally,
the poor suffer even more discrimination than Negroes in
criminal justice; and Negroes may suffer more from lack of
money than from race." "The Tipped Scales of American
Justice," in *Law and Order: The Scales of Justice*, ed., Abraham S. Blumberg (Aldine-Transaction, 1970), p. 40.

9. Isidore Silver, "Introduction" to the Avon edition of *The
Challenge of Crime in a Free Society* (New York: Avon Books,
1968), p. 31.

10. *Challenge*, p. 43. (Emphasis added.) The study referred to is
James S. Wallerstein and C. J. Wyle, "Our Law-abiding Law-
breakers," *Probation*, XXV (April, 1947), pp. 107-112.

11. This is the conclusion of Austin L. Porterfield, *Youth in Trouble* (Fort Worth: Leo Potishman Foundation, 1946); Fred J. Murphy, M. Shirley, and H. L. Witmer, "The Incidence of Hidden Delinquency," *American Journal of Orthopsychiatry*, XVI (October, 1946), pp. 686-96; James F. Short, Jr., "A Report on the Incidence of Criminal Behavior, Arrests, and Convictions in Selected Groups," *Proceedings of the Pacific Sociological Society*, 1954, pp. 110-18 [published as Vol XXII, No. 2, of *Research Studies of the State College of Washington* (Pullman, Washington, 1954)]; F. Ivan Nye, James F. Short, Jr. and Virgil J. Olson, "Socioeconomic Status and Delinquent Behavior," *American Journal of Sociology*, 63 (January, 1958), pp. 381-389; Maynard L. Erikson and Lamar T. Empey, "Class Position, Peers and Delinquency," *Sociology and Social Research*, 49 (April, 1965), pp. 268-282; William J. Chambliss and Richard H. Nagasawa, "On the Validity of Official Statistics— a Comparative Study of White, Black, and Japanese High-School Boys," *Journal of Research in Crime and Delinquency*, 6 (January, 1969), pp. 71-77; Eugene Doleschal, "Hidden Crime," *Crime and Delinquency Literature*, 2, No. 5 (October, 1970), pp. 546-572; Nanci Koser Wilson, *Risk Ratios in Juvenile Delinquency* (Ann Arbor, Michigan: University Microfilms, 1972); and Maynard L. Erikson, "Group Violations, Socioeconomic Status and Official Delinquency," *Social Forces*, 52, No. 1 (September, 1973), pp. 41-52.

12. This is the conclusion of Martin Gold, "Undetected Delinquent Behavior," *Journal of Research in Crime and Delinquency*, 3, No. 1 (1966), pp. 27-46; and of Sutherland and Cressey, *Criminology*, 9th edition (Philadelphia: Lippincott, 1974), pp. 137 and 220.

13. Cf. Larry Karacki and Jackson Toby, "The Uncommitted Adolescent: Candidate for Gang Socialization," *Sociological Inquiry*, 32 (1962), pp. 203-215; William R. Arnold, "Continuities in Research—Scaling Delinquent Behavior," *Social Problems*, 13, No. 1 (1965), pp. 59-66; Harwin L. Voss, "Socioeconomic Status and Reported Delinquent Behavior," *Social Problems*, 13, No. 3 (1966), pp. 314-324; LaMar Empey and Maynard L. Erikson, "Hidden Delinquency and Social Status," *Social Forces*, 44, No. 4 (1966), pp. 546-554; Fred J. Shanley, "Middle-class Delinquency as a Social Problem," *Sociology and Social Research*, 51 (1967), pp. 185-198; Jay R. Williams and Martin Gold, "From Delinquent Behavior to Official De-

linquency," *Social Problems,* 20, No. 2 (1972), pp. 209-229.
14. Empey and Erikson, "Hidden Delinquency and Social Status," pp. 549, 551. Nye, Short, and Olson also found destruction of property to be committed most frequently by upper-class boys and girls. "Socioeconomic Status and Delinquent Behavior," p. 385.
15. Op. cit., footnote 13, above.
16. Eugene Doleschal and Nora Klapmuts, "Toward a New Criminology," *Crime and Delinquency Literature,* 5 (December, 1973), p. 611.
17. Gold, "Undetected Delinquent Behavior," p. 37.
18. Ibid., p. 44. Doleschal, reviewing a later work of Martin Gold [*Delinquent Behavior in an American City* (Belmont, California: Brooks-Cole, 1970)], reports that "while the official figures on delinquency in Flint [Michigan] set the ratio of lower-class to middle-class delinquents at 8 to 1, Gold found that among the 20 percent most delinquent, there were about three lower-class boys for every two middle-class boys." Doleschal, "Hidden Crime," p. 556.
19. Comparing socioeconomic status categories "scant evidence is found that would support the contention that group delinquency is more characteristic of the lower-status levels than other socioeconomic status levels. . . . In fact, *only arrests seem to be more characteristic of the low-status category* than the other categories." Erikson, "Group Violations, Socioeconomic Status and Official Delinquency," p. 51. (Emphasis added.)
20. Gold, "Undetected Delinquent Behavior," p. 28. (Emphasis added.)
21. Ibid., p. 38.
22. Terence P. Thornberry, "Race, Socioeconomic Status and Sentencing in the Juvenile Justice System," *The Journal of Criminal Law and Criminology,* 64, No. 1 (1973), pp. 90-98.
23. Goldfarb, "Prisons: The National Poorhouse," p .17.
24. *UCR-1974,* p. 45. This was 41.2 percent in 1976. *UCR-1976,* p. 183.
25. Doleschal and Klapmuts, "Toward a New Criminology," p. 614, reporting the conclusions of Ross L. Purdy, *Factors in the Conviction of Law Violators: The Drinking Driver* (Ann Arbor, Michigan: University Microfilms, 1971).
26. Gerald Robin, "The Corporate and Judicial Disposition of Employee Thieves," *Wisconsin Law Review,* No. 3 (Summer, 1967), p. 693.
27. See for example D. Chapman, "The Stereotype of the Criminal

and the Social Consequences," *International Journal of Criminology and Penology*, 1, (1973), p. 24.

28. This view is widely held, although the degree to which it functions as a self-fulfilling prophecy is less widely recognized. Versions of this view can be seen in *Challenge*, p. 79; Jerome Skolnick, *Justice Without Trial* (New York: John Wiley, 1966), pp. 45-48, 217-218; and Jessica Mitford, *Kind and Usual Punishment*, p. 53. Piliavin and Briar write in "Police Encounters with Juveniles":

> Compared to other youths, Negroes and boys whose appearance matched the delinquent stereotype were more frequently stopped and interrogated by patrolmen—often even in the absence of evidence that an offense had been committed—usually were given more severe dispositions for the same violations. Our data suggest, however, that these selective apprehension and disposition practices resulted not only from the intrusion of long-held prejudices of individual police officers but also from certain job-related experiences of law-enforcement personnel. First, the tendency of police to give more severe dispositions to Negroes and to youths whose appearance correspond to that which police associated with delinquents partly reflected the fact, observed in this study, that these youths also were much more likely than were other types of boys to exhibit the sort of recalcitrant demeanor which police construed as a sign of the confirmed delinquent. Further, officers assumed, partly on the basis of departmental statistics, that Negroes and juveniles who "look tough" (e.g. who wear chinos, leather jackets, boots, etc.) commit crimes more frequently than do other types of youths. [p. 212]

Cf. Albert Reiss, *The Police and the Public* (New Haven, Yale University Press, 1971). Reiss attributes the differences to the differences in the actions of complainants.

29. Richard J. Lundman, for example, found higher arrest rates to be associated with "offender powerlessness." "Routine Police Arrest Practices: A Commonweal Perspective," *Social Problems*, 22, No. 1 (October, 1974), pp. 127-141.

30. Chamber of Commerce of the United States, *A Handbook on White Collar Crime* (Washington, D.C., 1974), p. 6. Copyright

© 1974 by the Chamber of Commerce of the United States. Reprinted by permission of the Chamber of Commerce of the United States.

31. Computed from figures in "Table 26—Offense Analysis 1974— Percent Distribution, Average Value, and Percent Change Over 1973," *UCR-1974*, p. 178.

32. *UCR-1974*, p. 178.

33. The President's Commission on Law Enforcement and Administration of Justice, *Task Force Report: Crime and Its Impact— an Assessment* (Washington, D.C.: U.S. Government Printing Office, 1967), pp. 103-104.

34. Gilbert Geis, "Upperworld Crime," in *Current Perspectives on Criminal Behavior*, ed., Abraham S. Blumberg (New York: Knopf, 1974), p. 126.

35. Sutherland and Cressey, *Criminology*, p. 41. (Emphasis added.)

36. *Task Force Report: Crime and Its Impact*, p. 107.

37. Hart, "Swindling and Knavery, Inc.," p. 158.

38. *Handbook on White Collar Crime*, p. 6.

39. *UCR-1974*, p. 179. This disparity increased considerably in 1976. See *UCR-1976*, p. 179.

40. See, for example, Theodore G. Chiricos, Phillip D. Jackson, and Gordon P. Waldo, "Inequality in the Imposition of a Criminal Label," *Social Problems*, 19, No. 4 (Spring, 1972), pp. 553-572.

41. Abraham S. Blumberg, *Criminal Justice* (Chicago: Quadrangle, 1967), p. 33. Even for the middle-class defendant, the state with its greater financial, investigatory, and legal personnel resources, holds the advantage over the accused— so the poor person is doubly disadvantaged. Cf. Abraham S. Goldstein, "The State and the Accused: Balance of Advantage in Criminal Procedure," in *Crime, Law and Society*, eds., Goldstein and Goldstein, pp. 173-206.

42. See, for example, C. E. Ares, A. Rankin, and J. H. Sturz, "The Manhattan Bail Project: An Interim Report on the Use of Pre-Trial Parole," *NYU Law Review*, 38 (1963), p. 67; C. Foote, "Compelling Appearances in Court-Administration of Bail in Philadelphia," *University of Pennsylvania Law Review*, 102 (1954), pp. 1031-79; and C. Foote, "A Study of the Administration of Bail in New York City," *University of Pennsylvania Law Review*, 106 (1958), p. 693. For statistics on persons held in jail awaiting trial, see *Black Population in the U.S.*, p. 171;

and U.S.L.E.A.A., *Survey of Inmates of Local Jails 1972—Advance Report* (Washington, D.C.: U.S. Government Printing Office, 1974), pp. 5 and 8.

43. Blumberg, *Criminal Justice*, pp. 28-29; *Challenge*, p. 134; and Donald J. Newman, *Conviction: The Determination of Guilt or Innocence Without Trial* (Boston: Little, Brown, 1966), p. 3.

44. A good summary of these developments can be found in Joel Jay Finer, "Ineffective Assistance of Counsel," *Cornell Law Review*, 58, No. 6 (July, 1973), pp. 1077-1120.

45. See, for example, Dallin H. Oaks and Warren Lehman, "Lawyers for the Poor," in *Law and Order: The Scales of Justice*, ed., A. Blumberg, pp. 92-93; also Jerome H. Skolnick, "Social Control in the Adversary System," in *Criminal Justice: Law and Politics*, ed., Cole (Belmont, California: Duxbury, 1972), p. 266. "The National Legal Aid and Defender Association has suggested that experienced attorneys handle no more than 150 felony cases per year, rather than . . . the case load of over 500 felony cases per attorney with which some public defender offices in major cities are burdened." Finer, "Ineffective Assistance of Counsel." (p. 1120)

46. In several essays, Abraham S. Blumberg has described the role of the public defender as an officer of the court bureaucracy rather than as a defender of the accused. See his "Lawyers with Convictions," in *Law and Order: The Scales of Justice*, pp. 51-67; "The Practice of Law as Confidence Game: Organizational Cooptation of a Profession," in *Criminal Law in Action*, ed., William J. Chambliss (Santa Barbara, California: Hamilton Publishing Co., 1975), pp. 262-275; and his book *Criminal Justice* (Chicago: Quadrangle, 1967), esp. pp. 13-115.

47. Jonathan D. Casper, "Did Your Have a Lawyer When You Went to Court? No, I Had a Public Defender," in *Criminal Justice: Law and Politics*, ed., Cole, pp. 239-240.

48. Blumberg, "Lawyers with Convictions," pp. 62-65; and his *Criminal Justice*, pp. 92-93.

49. Ibid.; percentages are rounded to nearest whole number.

50. Oaks and Lehman, "Lawyers for the Poor," p. 95.

51. Of those defendants who were *convicted* in U.S. District Courts in 1971, 46 percent had assigned lawyers (including public defenders); of those *acquitted*, 37.5 percent had assigned counsel; and of those *dismissed*, only 33.3 percent had assigned counsel. *Sourcebook*, p. 388.

52. Blake Fleetwood and Arthur Lubow, "America's Most Coddled

Criminals," *New Times* (September 19, 1975), pp. 26-29. *New Times Magazine*, copyright © 1975. Reprinted by permission of *New Times Magazine*.

53. Lesley Oelsner, "Wide Disparities Mark Sentences Here," *New York Times*, September 27, 1972, p. 1. Stuart Nagel writes, "The reasons for the economic class sentencing disparities, holding crime and prior record constant, are due possibly to the quality of legal representation that the indigent receive and probably to the appearance that an indigent defendant presents before a middle-class judge or probation officer." "Disparities in Sentencing Procedure," *UCLA Law Review*, 14 (August, 1967), p. 1283.

54. Oelsner, p. 1.

55. Nagel, "The Tipped Scales of American Justice," p. 39.

56. Doleschal and Klapmuts, "Toward a New Criminology," p. 613; reporting the findings of Terence Patrick Thornberry, *Punishment and Crime: The Effect of Legal Dispositions on Subsequent Criminal Behavior* (Ann Arbor, Michigan: University Microfilms, 1972); see footnote 22, above.

57. *Sourcebook*, pp. 333, 463, 443.

58. Henry Allen Bullock, "Significance of the Racial Factor in the Length of Prison Sentences," in *Crime and Justice in Society*, ed., R. Quinney (Boston: Little, Brown, 1969), p. 425.

59. William J. Chambliss and Robert B. Seidman, "Sentencing and Sentences," in *Criminal Law in Action*, ed., Chambliss, p. 339; reporting the findings of Mary Owen Cameron, *The Booster and the Snitch: Department Store Shoplifting* (New York: Free Press, 1964).

60. Marvin E. Wolfgang and Marc Riedel, "Race Judicial Discretion and the Death Penalty," in *Criminal Law in Action*, ed., Chambliss, p. 375.

61. Marvin E. Wolfgang, Arlene Kelly, and Hans C. Nolde, "Comparison of the Executed and the Commuted Among Admissions to Death Row," in *Crime and Justice in Society*, ed., Quinney, pp. 508, 513.

62. "Antitrust: Kauper's Last Stand," *Newsweek*, June 21, 1976, p. 70. On December 21, 1974, the "Antitrust Procedures and Penalty Act" was passed, striking out the language of the Sherman Antitrust Act, which made price-fixing a misdemeanor punishable by a maximum sentence of one year in prison. According to the new law, price-fixing is a felony punishable by up to three years in prison. Since prison senten-

ces were a rarity under the old law and usually involved only 30 days in jail when actually imposed, there is little reason to believe that the new law will strike fear in the hearts of corporate crooks.

63. *Task Force Report: Crime and Its Impact*, pp. 105, 106.

64. Marvin E. Frankel, *Criminal Sentences: Law Without Order* (New York: Hill and Wang, 1972), p. 24, footnote.

65. *Justice in Sentencing: Papers and Proceedings of the Sentencing Institute for the First and Second U.S. Judicial Circuits*, eds., Leonard Orland and Harold R. Tyler, Jr. (Mineola, New York: Foundation Press, 1974), pp. 159-160. (Emphasis added.)

66. Michael C. Jensen, "Watergate Donors Still Riding High," *The New York Times*, August 24, 1975, sec. 3, pp. 1, 7. Copyright © 1975 by The New York Times Company. Reprinted by permission.

67. Tom Wicker, *A Time to Die* (New York: Quadrangle, 1975), pp. 311, 314.

68. Ibid., p. 310.

69. *Sourcebook*, p. 470.

70. U.S. Department of Justice, U.S. Law Enforcement Assistance Administration, National Criminal Justice Information and Statistics Service, *Survey of Inmates of Local Jails: Advance Report* (Washington, D.C.: U.S. Government Printing Office, 1974), pp. 3, 4, 16.

71. U.S. Department of Justice, U.S. Law Enforcement Assistance Administration, National Criminal Justice Information and Statistics Service, *Survey of Inmates of State Correctional Facilities, 1974*, No. SD-NPS-SR-2 (Washington, D.C.: U.S. Government Printing Office, March, 1976), pp. 1, 2, 4, 5, 6, 9, and 25.

4

To the Vanquished Belong the Spoils: Who Is Winning the Losing War Against Crime?

*In every case the laws are made by the
ruling party in its own interest; a
democracy makes democratic laws, a
despot autocratic ones, and so on. By
making these laws they define as "just"
for their subjects whatever is for their own
interest, and they call anyone who breaks
them a "wrongdoer" and punish him
accordingly.*

Thrasymachus, in Plato's *Republic*

a. Why Is the Criminal Justice System Failing?

The streams of my argument flow together at this point in a
question: *Why is it happening?* I have shown that the criminal justice system seems bent on failing to reduce crime,
bent on closing its eyes to the dangerous acts of the affluent,
bent on stacking the deck against the poor. I have shown
how the criminal justice system is biased at every stage, so
that it does not apprehend and punish a fair representation
of the individuals who are dangerous to society but primarily

apprehends and punishes only the poor among those who are dangerous to society while letting the affluent who pose an equal or greater threat go free or get off lightly. I have shown how it is no accident that "the offender at the end of the road in prison is likely to be a member of the lowest social and economic groups in the country."[1] I have shown that this is not an accurate group portrait of who threatens society—it is a picture of who the criminal justice system *selects* for arrest and imprisonment from among those who threaten society. It is an image distorted by the shape of the criminal justice carnival mirror.

This much we have seen and now we want to know why: *Why is the criminal justice system allowed to function in a fashion that neither protects society nor achieves justice?*[2] *Why is the criminal justice system failing in the way that it is?*

My answer to these questions is a simple one: *The failure of the criminal justice system serves the interests of the rich and powerful in America.* From their viewpoint, *nothing succeeds like failure.*

The "failure" of criminal justice has two aspects. First, there is a real (and growing) threat of crime. This is due in part to our failure to implement policies that could reduce crime. Second, our jails and prisons and thus our newspapers and newscasts are filled with poor people who are being punished for this crime. This is due to the bias built into the system from start to finish. *The result of these factors in combination is that an image is vividly conveyed to the American people: there is a real threat of crime and it is a threat from the poor.*

This image serves the interests of the rich and powerful in America. It carries an *ideological message* that serves to protect their wealth and privilege. Crudely put, the message is this:

- *The threat to "law-abiding middle America" comes from below them on the economic ladder, not above them.*
- *The poor are morally defective, and thus their poverty is*

*their own fault, not a symptom of social or economic
injustice.*

The effect of these messages is to funnel the discontent of
middle Americans into hostility toward, and fear of, the poor.
It leads Americans to ignore the ways in which they are injured and ripped off by the acts of the affluent (as catalogued
in Chapter 2) and leads them to demand harsher doses of
"law and order" aimed mainly at the lower classes. Most
importantly, it nudges middle America toward a *conservative* defense of American society with its vast disparities of
wealth, power, and opportunity—and nudges them away
from a *radical* demand for equality and an equitable distribution of wealth and power. In sum, *the failure of the
criminal justice system is allowed because it performs an
ideological service for those with the power to change the
system.*

On the other hand, but of equal importance, is the fact that
those who are truly victimized by the "failure" to reduce
crime are by and large the poor themselves. That is, those
people who are most hurt by the failure of the criminal justice
system are those with the least power to change the system.
A poor black is 25 times more likely than a wealthy white to
be a victim of robbery with serious assault. A poor black has
a 1-in-100 chance of being injured by aggravated assault
annually, while a wealthy white has a 1-in-700 chance.[3] The
poor are also disproportionately hurt by property crimes.
They are far less likely than the affluent to have insurance
against theft, and since they have little to start with, what
they lose to theft takes a much deeper bite into their ability
to meet their basic needs.

Those who are really hurt by the failure to reduce crime are
not in a position to change criminal justice policy. Those who
are in a position to change criminal justice policy are not
seriously harmed by its failure—and, furthermore, there are
actual benefits to them from that failure.

*This is why the criminal justice system is allowed to fail in
the way it does.* It is important to note that this is in no way

a "conspiracy theory." I am not claiming that the powerful in America consciously sabotage the war on crime in order to secure ideological benefits. My point is more complex. Those who are hurt by present criminal justice policy, who really would have an incentive to change it, are not in a position to do so. Those who are in a position to change criminal justice policy find themselves in a situation of little loss and much benefit and thus have no incentive to change it.

My argument in the remainder of this chapter takes the following form. In section b, "The Poverty of Criminals and the Crime of Poverty," I spell out the content of the ideological message broadcast by the failure of the criminal justice system. In section c, "Ideology, or How to Fool Enough of the People Enough of the Time," I discuss the *nature* of ideology in general, the *need* for it in America, and the *willingness* of our leaders to use criminal justice institutions to serve their interests rather than the public's. Section c then sketches out—often only in rough outline—the larger philosophical and political context in which the material in section b is to be understood. Ultimately, however, the test of the argument in this chapter, setting out the interests served by the present biased dysfunctioning of the criminal justice system, is whether or not it provides a plausible explanation of the failure of criminal justice and draws the arguments of the previous chapters together into a coherent theory of contemporary criminal justice policy and practice.

b. The Poverty of Criminals and the Crime of Poverty

Criminal justice is a very visible part of the American scene. As fact and fiction, countless images of crime and the struggle against it assail our senses daily, even hourly. In *every* newspaper, in *every* TV or radio newscast, there is at least one criminal justice story and often more. It is as if we live in an embattled city, besieged by the forces of crime and bravely defended by the forces of the law—and as we go about our daily tasks, we are always conscious of the war raging not very far away; newspapers bring us daily, and newscasts bring us hourly, reports from the "front." Between reports, we are vividly reminded of the stakes and the desperateness of the battle by fictionalized portrayals of the struggle between the forces of the law and the breakers of the law. There is scarcely an hour on TV without some dramatization of the struggle against crime. (In the *TV Guide* for the week of June 26 through July 2, 1976, there are listed *133 programs* dramatically portraying the struggle against crime. Keep in mind that there are 168 hours in a week, and TV stations do not broadcast all around the clock! Keep in mind also that 98 percent of American homes have televisions, and it is estimated that they are on an average of six hours a day![4]) If we add to this the news accounts, the panel discussions, and the political speeches about crime, there can be no doubt that, as fact or fancy or both, criminal justice is vividly present in the imaginations of most Americans.

And this is no accident. Everyone can relate to criminal justice in personal and emotional terms. Everyone has some fear of crime, and, as we saw in Chapter 3, just about everyone has committed some. And everyone knows the primitive satisfaction of seeing justice done and the evildoers served up their just deserts. Furthermore, in reality or in fiction, criminal justice is naturally dramatic. It contains the acts of courage and cunning, the high risks and high stakes, and the life-and-death struggle between good and evil that are missing from the routine lives so many of us lead. To identify with the struggle against crime is to expand one's experience vicariously to include the danger, the suspense, the triumphs, the meaningfulness—in a word, the drama—often missing in ordinary life. How else can we explain the seemingly bottomless appetite Americans have for the endless repetition, in only slightly altered form, of the same theme: the struggle of the forces of law against the forces of crime? There can be no getting away from the fact that criminal justice has a firm grip on the imaginations of Americans and is thus in a unique position *to convey a message to Americans and to convey it with drama and with conviction.*

Let us now look at this message in detail. Our task falls naturally into two parts. There is an ideological message, a message supportive of the status quo, built into *any* criminal justice system by its very nature. Even if the criminal justice system were not failing, even if it were not biased against the poor, it would still—by its very nature—broadcast a message supportive of established institutions. This is *the implicit ideology of criminal justice.* Beyond this, there is an additional ideological message conveyed by the *failure* of the system and by its *biased* concentration on the poor. I call this the *bonus of bias.* The combination of this bonus with the ideology always implicit in criminal justice yields the powerful ideological message broadcast by the failure of the criminal justice system. Let us turn now to the elements of this combination.

1.   The Implicit Ideology of Criminal Justice

Every criminal justice system conveys a subtle, yet powerful message in support of established institutions. It does this for two interconnected reasons.

First, because it concentrates on *individual* wrongdoers. This means that it *diverts our attention away from our institutions, away from consideration of whether our institutions themselves are wrong or unjust or indeed "criminal."*

Second, because the criminal law is put forth as the *minimum neutral ground rules* for any social living. We are taught that no society can exist without rules against theft and violence, and thus the criminal law is put forth as politically neutral, as the minimum requirements for *any* society, as the minimum obligations that any individual owes his fellows to make social life of any decent sort possible. Thus, it not only diverts our attention away from the possible injustice of our social institutions, but *the criminal law bestows upon those institutions the mantle of its own neutrality.*

DIVERT
ATTNS.

Since the criminal law protects the established institutions (e.g., the prevailing economic arrangements are protected by laws against theft, etc.), attacks on those established institutions become equivalent to violations of the minimum requirements for any social life at all. In effect, *the criminal law enshrines the established institutions as equivalent to the minimum requirements for **any** decent social existence—and it brands the individual who attacks those institutions as one who has declared war on **all** organized society and who must therefore be met with the weapons of war.*

This is the powerful magic of criminal justice. By virtue of its focus on *individual* criminals, it diverts us from the evils of the *social* order. By virtue of its presumed neutrality, it transforms the established social (and economic) order from being merely *one* form of society open to critical comparison with others into *the* conditions of *any* social order and thus immune from criticism. Let us look more closely at this process.

What is the effect of focusing on individual guilt? Not only does this divert our attention from the possible evils in our institutions, but it puts forth half the problem of justice as if it were the *whole* problem. To focus on individual guilt is to ask whether or not the individual citizen has fulfilled his obligations to his fellow citizens. *It is to look away from the issue of whether his fellow citizens have fulfilled their obligations to him.*

To look only at individual responsibility is to look away from social responsibility. To look only at individual criminality is to close one's eyes to social injustice and to close one's ears to the question of whether our social institutions have exploited or violated the individual. *Justice is a two-way street—but criminal justice is a one-way street.*

Individuals owe obligations to their fellow citizens because their fellow citizens owe obligations to them. Criminal justice focuses on the first and looks away from the second. *Thus, by focusing on individual responsibility for crime, the criminal justice system literally acquits the existing social order of any charge of injustice!*

This is an extremely important bit of ideological alchemy. It stems from the fact the same act can be criminal or not, unjust or just, depending on the conditions in which it takes place. Killing someone is ordinarily a crime. But if it is in self-defense or to stop a deadly crime, it is not. Taking property by force is usually a crime. But if the taking is just retrieving what has been stolen, then no crime has been committed. Acts of violence are ordinarily crimes. But if the violence is provoked by the threat of violence or by oppressive conditions, then, like the Boston Tea Party, what might ordinarily be called criminal is celebrated as just. This means that when we call an act a crime *we are also making an implicit judgment about the conditions in response to which it takes place.* When we call an act a crime, we are saying that the conditions in which it occurs are not themselves criminal or deadly or oppressive or so unjust as to make an extreme response reasonable or justified, that is, to make such a response noncriminal.

This means that when the system holds an individual responsible for a crime, *it is implicitly conveying the message that the social conditions in which the crime occurred are not responsible for the crime,* that they are not so unjust as to make a violent response to them excusable. The criminal justice system conveys as much by what it does not do as by what it does. By holding the individual responsible, *it literally acquits the society of criminality or injustice.*

Judges are prone to hold than an individual's responsibility for a violent crime is diminished if it was provoked by something that might lead a "reasonable man" to respond violently and that criminal responsibility is eliminated if the act was in response to conditions so intolerable that any "reasonable man" would have been likely to respond in the same way. In this vein, the law acquits those who kill or injure in self-defense and treats lightly those who commit a crime when confronted with extreme provocation. The law treats leniently the man who kills his wife's lover and the woman who kills her brutal husband, even when neither has acted directly in self-defense. By this logic, when we hold an individual completely responsible for a crime, we are saying that the conditions in which it occurred are such that a "reasonable man" should find them tolerable. In other words, by focusing on individual responsibility for crimes, *the criminal justice system broadcasts the message that the social order itself is reasonable and not intolerably unjust.*

Thus the criminal justice system serves to focus moral condemnation on individuals and to deflect it away from the social order that may have either violated the individual's rights or dignity or literally pushed him or her to the brink of crime. This not only serves to carry the message that our social institutions are not in need of fundamental questioning, but it further suggests that the justice of our institutions is obvious, not to be doubted. Indeed, since it is deviations from these institutions that are crimes, the established institutions become the implicit standard of justice from which criminal deviations are measured.

This leads to the second way in which a criminal justice system always conveys an implicit ideology. It arises from the presumption that the criminal law is nothing but the politically neutral minimum requirements of any decent social life. What is the consequence of this?

Obviously, as already suggested, this presumption transforms the prevailing social order into justice incarnate and all violations of the prevailing order into injustice incarnate. This process is so obvious that it may be easily missed.

Consider, for example, the law against theft. It does indeed seem to be one of the minimum requirements of social living. As long as there is scarcity, any society—capitalist or socialist—will need rules preventing individuals from taking what does not belong to them. But the law against theft is more: it is a law against stealing what individuals *presently* own. *Such a law has the effect of making present property relations a part of the criminal law.*

Since stealing is a violation of law, this means that present property relations become the implicit standard of justice against which criminal deviations are measured. Since criminal law is thought of as the minimum requirements of any social life, this means that present property relations become equivalent to the minimum requirements of *any* social life. And the criminal who would alter the present property relations becomes nothing less than someone who is declaring war on all organized society. The question of whether this "war" is provoked by the injustice or brutality of the society is swept aside. Indeed, this suggests yet another way in which the criminal justice system conveys an ideological message in support of the established society.

Not only does the criminal justice system acquit the social order of any charge of injustice, it specifically cloaks the society's own crime-producing tendencies. I have already observed that by blaming the individual for a crime, the society is acquitted of the charge of injustice. I would like to go further now and argue that by blaming the individual for a crime, the society is acquitted of the charge of complicity in that crime! This is a point worth developing, since many observers have maintained that modern competitive societies such as our own have structural features that tend to generate crime. Thus, holding the individual responsible for his or her crime serves the function of taking the rest of society off the hook for their role in sustaining and benefiting from social arrangements that produce crime. Let us take a brief detour to look more closely at this process.

Cloward and Ohlin argue in their book *Delinquency and Opportunity*[5] that much crime is the result of the discrepancy between social goals and the legitimate opportunities available for achieving them. Simply put, in our society everyone is encouraged to be a success, but the avenues to success are open only to some. The conventional wisdom of our free enterprise democracy is that anyone can be a success if he or she has the talent and the ambition. Thus, if one is not a success, it is because of their own shortcomings: laziness or lack of ability or both. On the other hand, opportunities to achieve success are not equally open to all. Access to the best schools and the best jobs is effectively closed to all but a few of the poor and begins to open wider only as one goes up the economic ladder. The result is that many are called but few are chosen. And many who have taken the bait and accepted the belief in the importance of success and the belief that achieving success is a result of individual ability must cope with the feelings of frustration and failure that result when they find the avenues to success closed. Cloward and Ohlin argue that one method of coping with these stresses is to develop alternative avenues to success. Crime is such an alternative avenue. Crime is a means by which people who believe in the American dream pursue it when they find the traditional routes barred. Indeed, it is plain to see that the goals pursued by most criminals are as American as apple pie. I suspect that one of the reasons that American moviegoers enjoy gangster films—movies in which gangsters such as Al Capone, Bonnie and Clyde, or Butch Cassidy and the Sundance Kid are the heroes, as distinct from police and detective films whose heroes are defenders of the law—is that even where they deplore the hero's methods, they identify with his or her notion of success, since it is theirs as well, and respect the courage and cunning displayed in achieving that success.

It is important to note that the discrepancy between success goals and legitimate opportunities in America is not an aberration. It is a structural feature of modern competitive industrialized society, a feature from which many benefits flow. Cloward and Ohlin write that

> a crucial problem in the industrial world... is to locate and train the most talented persons in every generation, irrespective of the vicissitudes of birth, to occupy technical work roles.... Since we cannot know in advance who can best fulfill the requirements of the various occupational roles, the matter is presumably settled through the process of competition. But how can men throughout the social order be motivated to participate in this competition?...
>
> One of the ways in which the industrial society attempts to solve this problem is by defining success-goals as potentially accessible to all, regardless of race, creed, or socioeconomic position.[6]

But since these universal goals are urged to encourage a competition to weed out the best, there are necessarily fewer openings than seekers. And since those who achieve success are in a particularly good position to exploit their success to make access for their own children easier, the competition is rigged to work in favor of the middle and upper classes. As a result, "many lower-class persons...are the victims of a contradiction between the goals toward which they have been led to orient themselves and socially structured means of striving for these goals."[7]

> [The poor] experience desperation born of the certainty that their position in the economic structure is realtively fixed and immutable—a desperation made all the more poignant by their exposure to a cultural ideology in which failure to orient oneself upward is regarded as a moral defect and failure to become mobile as proof of it.[8]

The outcome is predictable. "Under these conditions, there is an acute pressure to depart from institutional norms and to adopt illegitimate alternatives."[9]

In brief, this means that the very way in which our society is structured to draw out the talents and energies that go into producing our high standard of living has a costly side effect: it produces crime. But by holding individuals responsible for this crime, those who enjoy that high standard of living can have their cake and eat it. They can reap the benefits of the competition for success and escape the responsibility of paying for the costs of that competition. By holding the poor crook legally and morally guilty, the rest of society not only passes the costs of competition on to the poor, but they effectively deny that they (the affluent) are the beneficiaries of an economic system that exacts such a high toll in frustration and suffering.

Willem Bonger, the Dutch Marxist criminologist, maintained that competitive capitalism produces egotistic motives and undermines compassion for the misfortunes of others and thus makes human beings literally *more capable of crime*—more capable of preying on their fellows without moral inhibition or remorse—than earlier cultures that emphasized cooperation rather than competition.[10] Here again, the criminal justice system relieves those who benefit from the American economic system of the costs of that system. By holding criminals morally and individually responsible for their crimes, we can forget that the motives that lead to crime—the drive for success at any cost, linked with the beliefs that success means outdoing others and that violence is an acceptable way of achieving one's goals—are the same motives that powered the drive across the American continent and that continue to fuel the engine of America's prosperity.

David Gordon, a contemporary political economist, maintains "that nearly all crimes in capitalist societies represent perfectly *rational* responses to the structure of institutions upon which capitalist societies are based."[11] That is, like Bonger, Gordon believes that capitalism tends to provoke crime in all economic strata. This is so because most crime is motivated by a desire for property or money and is an understandable way of coping with the pressures of inequality, competition, and insecurity, all of which are essential ingredients of capitalism. Capitalism depends, Gordon writes,

on basically competitive forms of social and economic interaction and upon substantial inequalities in the allocation of social resources. Without inequalities, it would be much more difficult to induce workers to work in alienating environments. Without competition and a competitive ideology, workers might not be inclined to struggle to improve their relative income and status in society by working harder. Finally, although rights of property are protected, capitalist societies do not guarantee economic security to most of their individual members. Individuals must fend for themselves, finding the best available opportunities to provide for themselves and their families.... Driven by the fear of economic insecurity and by a competitive desire to gain some of the goods unequally distributed throughout the society, many individuals will eventually become "criminals."[12]

To the extent that a society makes crime a reasonable alternative for a large number of its members from all classes, that society is itself not very reasonably or humanely organized and bears some degree of responsibility for the crime it encourages. Since the criminal law is put forth as the minimum requirements that can be expected of any "reasonable man," its enforcement amounts to a denial of the real nature of the social order to which Gordon and the others point. Here again, by blaming the individual criminal, the criminal justice system serves implicitly but dramatically to acquit the society of its criminality.

2. The Bonus of Bias

We turn now to consideration of the additional ideological bonus that is derived from the criminal justice system's bias against the poor. This bonus is a product of the association of crime and poverty in the popular mind. This association, the merging of the "criminal classes" and the "lower classes" into the "dangerous classes," was not invented in America. The word "villain" is derived from the Latin *villanus*, which means a farm servant. And the term "villein" was used in feudal England to refer to a serf who farmed the land of a great lord and who was literally owned by that lord.[13] In this respect, our present criminal justice system is heir to a long and hallowed tradition.

The value of this association was already seen when we explored the "average citizen's" concept of the Typical Criminal and the Typical Crime. It is quite obvious that throughout the great mass of middle America, far more fear and hostility is directed toward the predatory acts of the poor than the rich. Compare the fate of politicians in recent history who call for tax reform, income redistribution, prosecution of corporate crime, and any sort of regulation of business that would make it better serve American social goals with that of politicians who erect their platform on a call for "law and order," more police, less limits on police power, and stiffer prison sentences for criminals—and consider this in light of what we have already seen about the real dangers posed by corporate crime and business-as-usual.

In view of all that has been said already, it seems clear that Americans have been systematically deceived as to what are the greatest dangers to their lives, limbs and possessions. The very persistence with which the system functions to apprehend and punish poor crooks and ignore or slap on the wrist equally or more dangerous individuals is testimony to the sticking power of this deception. That Americans continue to tolerate the gentle treatment meted out to white-collar criminals, corporate price fixers, industrial polluters, and political-influence peddlers, while voting in droves to lock up more poor people faster and longer, indicates the degree to which they harbor illusions as to who most threatens them. It is perhaps also part of the explanation for the continued dismal failure of class-based politics in America. American workers rarely seem able to forget their differences and unite to defend their shared interests against the rich whose wealth they produce. Ethnic divisions serve this divisive function well, but undoubtedly the vivid portrayal of the poor—and, of course, the blacks—as hovering birds of prey waiting for the opportunity to snatch away the workers' meager gains serves also to deflect opposition away from the upper classes. A politician who promises to keep their communities free of blacks and their prisons full of them can get their votes even if the major portion of his or her policies amount to continuation of favored treatment of the rich at their expense. Surely this is a minor miracle of mind control.

The most important "bonus" derived from the identification of crime and poverty is that it paints the picture that the threat to decent middle Americans comes from those below them on the economic ladder, not those above. For this to happen the system must not only identify crime and poverty, but *it must also fail to reduce crime so that it remains a real threat.* By doing this, it deflects the fear and discontent of middle Americans, and their possible opposition, away from the wealthy. The two politicians who most clearly gave voice to the discontent of middle Americans in the post-World War II period were George Wallace and Spiro Agnew. Is it any accident that their politics was extremely conservative and their anger reserved for the poor (the welfare chiselers) and the criminal (the targets of law and order)?

There are other bonuses as well. For instance, if the criminal justice system functions to send out a message that bestows legitimacy on present property relations, the dramatic impact is mightily enhanced if the violator of the present arrangements is propertyless. In other words, the crimes of the well-to-do "redistribute" property among the haves. In that sense, they do not pose a symbolic challenge to the larger system in which some have much and many have little or nothing. If the criminal threat can be portrayed as coming from the poor, then the punishment of the poor criminal becomes a morality play in which the sanctity and legitimacy of the system in which some have plenty and others have little or nothing is dramatically affirmed. It matters little who the poor criminals really rip off. What counts is that middle Americans come to fear that those poor criminals are out to steal what they own.

There is yet another and, I believe, still more important bonus for the powerful in America, produced by the identification of crime and poverty. It might be thought that the identification of crime and poverty would produce sympathy for the criminals. My suspicion is that it produces or at least reinforces the reverse: *hostility toward the poor.*

Indeed, there is little evidence that Americans are very sympathetic to criminals or poor people. I have already pointed to the fact that very few Americans believe poverty to be a cause of crime. Other surveys find that most Americans believe that police should be tougher than they are now in dealing with crime (83 percent of those questioned in a 1972 survey); that courts do not deal harshly enough with criminals (75 percent of those questioned in a 1969 survey);

that a majority of Americans would like to see the death
penalty for convicted murderers (57 percent of those questioned in November 1972); and that most would be more likely to vote for a candidate who advocated tougher sentences
for lawbreakers (83 percent of those questioned in a 1972 survey).[14] Indeed, the experience of Watergate seems to suggest
that sympathy for criminals begins to flower only when we
approach the higher reaches of the ladder of wealth and
power. For some poor ghetto youth who robs a liquor store,
five years in the slammer is our idea of tempering justice with
mercy. When a handful of public officials try to walk off with
the U.S. Constitution, a few months in a minimum security
prison will suffice. If the public official is high enough, resignation from office and public disgrace tempered with a
$60,000-a-year pension is punishment enough.

My view is that since the criminal justice system—in fact
and fiction—deals with *individual legal* and *moral guilt*, the
association of crime with poverty does not mitigate the
image of individual moral responsibility for crime, the image
that crime is the result of an individual's poor character. My
suspicion is that it does the reverse: it generates the association of poverty and individual moral failing and thus *the
belief that poverty itself is a sign of poor or weak character.*
The clearest evidence that Americans hold this belief is to be
found in the fact that attempts to aid the poor are regarded as
acts of charity rather than as acts of justice. Our welfare system has all the demeaning attributes of an institution designed to give handouts to the undeserving and none of the
dignity of an institution designed to make good on our
responsibilities to our fellow human beings. If we acknowledged the degree to which our economic and social institutions themselves breed poverty, we would have to recognize
our own responsibilities toward the poor. If we can convince
ourselves that the poor are poor because of their own shortcomings, particularly moral shortcomings like incontinence
and indolence, then we need acknowledge no such responsibility to the poor. Indeed, we can go further and pat ourselves
on the back for our generosity in handing out the little that

we do, and of course, we can make our recipients go through all the indignities that mark them as the undeserving objects of our benevolence. By and large, this has been the way in which Americans have dealt with their poor.[15] It is a way that enables us to avoid asking the question of why the richest nation in the world continues to produce massive poverty. It is my view that this conception of the poor is subtly conveyed by the way our criminal justice system functions.

Obviously, no ideological message could be more supportive of the present social and economic order than this. It suggests that poverty is a sign of individual failing, not a symptom of social or economic injustice. It tells us loud and clear that massive poverty in the midst of abundance is not a sign pointing toward the need for fundamental changes in our social and economic institutions. It suggests that the poor are poor because they deserve to be poor, or at least because they lack the strength of character to overcome poverty. When the poor are seen to be poor in character, then economic poverty coincides with moral poverty and the economic order coincides with the moral order—as if a divine hand guided its workings, capitalism leads to everyone getting what they morally deserve!

If this association takes root, then when the poor individual is found guilty of a crime, the criminal justice system acquits the society of its responsibility not only for crime *but for poverty as well.*

With this, the ideological message of criminal justice is complete. The poor rather than the rich are seen as the enemies of the mass of decent middle Americans. Our social and economic institutions are held to be responsible for neither crime nor poverty and thus are in need of no fundamental questioning or reform. The poor are poor because they are poor of character. The economic order and the moral order are one. And to the extent that this message sinks in, the wealthy can rest easily—even if they cannot sleep the sleep of the just.

Thus, we can understand why the criminal justice system creates the image of crime as the work of the poor and fails

to stem it so that the threat of crime remains real and cred-
ible. The result is ideological alchemy of the highest order.
The poor are seen as the real threat to decent society. The
ultimate sanctions of criminal justice dramatically sanctify
the present social and economic order, and *the poverty of
criminals makes poverty itself an individual moral crime!*

Such are the ideological fruits of a losing war against
crime whose distorted image is reflected in the criminal justice carnival mirror and widely broadcast to reach the minds
and imaginations of America.

c. Ideology, or How to Fool Enough of the People Enough of the Time

1. What Is Ideology?

The view that the laws of a state or nation are made to serve
the interests of those with power, rather than to promote the
well-being of the whole society, is not a new discovery made
in the wake of Watergate. It is a doctrine with a pedigree
older even than Christianity itself. Writing during the fourth
century B.C., virtually at the dawn of western thought, Plato
expressed this view through the lips of Thrasymachus.[16] A
more contemporary and more systematic formulation of the
idea is found in the works of Karl Marx. Writing during the
nineteenth century, not long after the dawn of western indus-
trialism, Marx wrote in *The Communist Manifesto* that the
bourgeoisie—the class of owners of businesses and factories,
the class of capitalists—has

> conquered for itself, in the modern representative State, ex-
> clusive political sway. The executive of the modern State is but
> a committee for managing the common affairs of the whole
> bourgeoisie.[17]

Anyone who thinks this is a ridiculous idea ought to look at
the backgrounds of our political leaders. The vast majority of

the members of the president's cabinet, of the administrators of the federal regulatory agencies, and of the members of the two houses of Congress come from the ranks of business or of the lawyers who serve business. Many still maintain their business ties or law practices, with no sense of a conflict of interest with their political role.[18] If either Thrasymachus or Marx is right, there *is* no conflict with their political role, since that role is to protect and promote the interests of business.

Marx, of course, went further. Not only are the laws of a society made to protect the interests of the most powerful economic class, Marx argued that the prevailing ways of thinking about the world—from economic theory to religion to conventional moral ideas about good and evil, guilt and responsibility—are shaped to promote the belief that the existing society is the best of all possible worlds. Marx wrote that

> the ideas of the ruling class are in every epoch the ruling ideas: i.e. the class which is the ruling *material* force of society, is at the same time its ruling *intellectual* force. The class which has the means of material production at its disposal, has control at the same time over the means of mental production.[19]

In simple terms, because those who have economic power (i.e., those who have control over the means of material production) own the newspapers, endow the universities, finance the publication of books and journals, and (in our own time) control the television and radio industries, they have a prevailing say in what is said, heard, and thought by (i.e., they have control over the means of mental production for) the millions who get their ideas—their picture of reality—from these sources.

Even in a society such as ours, where freedom of expression has reached a level probably unparalleled in history, there is almost never any *fundamental* questioning of our political-economic-legal institutions in the mass media, that is, TV and radio, the major newspapers, or the news weeklies such as *Time* or *Newsweek*. There is criticism of individuals and of individual policies aplenty. But how often does one find the mass media questioning whether the free enterprise system is really the best choice for America or whether our political and legal arrangements systematically promote the domination of society by the owners of big business? These issues are rarely if ever raised. Instead, it is taken for granted that, although they need some reform tinkering from time to time, our economic institutions are the most productive, our political institutions the most free, and our legal institutions the most just *there can be.*

In other words, even in a society as free as ours, the ideas that are generally broadcast in society, the ideas that fill the heads and shape the picture of reality held by most Americans, either explicitly or implicitly convey the message that our leaders are pursuing the common good (with only occasional lapses into personal venality—note how we congratulate ourselves on how "the system is working" when we expose these "aberrations" and then return to business as usual) and that the interests of the powerful coincide with the common interests of us all[20]—that "what's good for General Motors is good for the country." When ideas are used explicitly to justify the power and privileges of those who rule the society or are used implicitly to justify them by taking for granted the sanctity of the social order and conveying the message that it is unnecessary or foolish to question it, we have what Marx called *ideology.*[21]

Marx's notion of ideology is a more respectable but not-so-distant cousin of the concept of *propaganda.* Both connote the use of ideas to achieve a political goal instead of to achieve truth. Both connote sham or deception, since an idea cannot be used to promote a political goal if it is admitted that this is why it is being put forth. Propaganda cannot work if it begins with the announcement: the following message is propaganda. The same is true for ideology.

Both ideology and propaganda are thus necessarily deceptions, perversions of the natural function of ideas, distortions of reality in the service of political goals. Propaganda is less respectable than ideology because it always suggests the conscious intention to deceive. A propagandist is some-

one like Tokyo Rose who intentionally lies to promote a political aim. Ideology may or may not be conscious. People may
spout ideology simply because it is all they know or all they
have been taught or because they do not see beyond the "conventional wisdom" that surrounds them. This can be just as
true of scholars who fail to see beyond the conventional assumptions of their disciplines as it is of laymen who fail to
see beyond the oversimplifications of what is commonly
called "common sense." Such individuals do not mouth an
ideology out of a willful desire to deceive and manipulate
their fellows but rather because their own view of reality is
distorted by untruths or half-truths. Thus, the deceptions of
ideology are less personally wicked but more socially insid-
ious than the deceptions of propaganda.

It should be noted in passing that not everyone uses the
term "ideology" as I have, to point to what is necessarily
deceptive. Some writers speak of ideology as if it meant any
individual or group's "belief system" or "value system" or
Weltanschauung, that is, "worldview."[22] I do not intend to
quibble about semantics. However, such a moral neutraliza-
tion of the concept of "ideology" strikes me as unnecessarily
dulling an instrument that thinkers like Marx and others
have sharpened into an effective tool for cutting through the
illusions that dog our political life. Such tools are few and
hard to find. Once found, they should be carefully preserved,
especially when concepts such as "belief system" or "worldview" are available to perform the more neutral function.
When I speak of ideology, I mean *the conscious or uncon-
scious use of ideas* (or images or other "messages"), *not for
the purpose of conveying the truth, but falsely to justify* (or
legitimate) *the prevailing distribution of power and wealth
and thus to secure allegiance to* (or undermine opposition to)
*the social order characterized by that distribution of power
and wealth.*

2.   The Need for Ideology

An argument that is both simple and persuasive can be made
for the claim that the rich and powerful in America have an

interest in conveying an ideological message to the rest of the nation. The argument is this. The have-nots and have-littles far outnumber the have-plenties. This means, to put it rather crudely, the have-nots and the have-littles could have more if they decided to take it from the have-plenties. This, in turn, means that the have-plenties need the cooperation of the have-nots and the have-littles. And since the have-plenties are such a small minority that they could never *force* this cooperation on the have-nots and have-littles, this coopera- tion must be voluntary. And for the cooperation to be volun- tary, the have-nots and the have-littles must believe that it would not be right or reasonable to take away what the have- plenties have. In other words, they must believe that for all its problems the present social, political, and economic order, with its disparities of wealth and power and privilege, is about the best that human beings can do. More specifically, the have-nots and have-littles must believe that they are not being ripped off by the have-plenties. Now this seems to me to add up to an extremely plausible argument that those in con- trol of our nation's institutions and media (i.e., the have- plenties) will have plenty of reason (if not an irresistable temptation) to shape those institutions and use those media in ways that support the beliefs necessary to secure the vol- untary acquiescence of the less well-off majority. And these beliefs must be in some considerable degree false, since the distribution of wealth and power in the United States is so evidently arbitrary and unjust. Ergo, the need for ideology.

A disquisition on the inequitable distribution of wealth and income in the United States is beyond the scope and pur- pose of this book. This subject, as well as the existence of a "dominant" or "ruling" class in America, has been docu- mented extensively by others.[23] I will only make two points here and make them briefly. First, there are indeed wide dis- parities in the distribution of wealth and income in the United States. Second, these disparities are so obviously un- just that it is reasonable to assume that the vast majority of people who must struggle to make ends meet only put up with them because they have been sold a bill of goods, that is, an ideology.

Studying the latest year for which complete data were available, Brookings economists Pechman and Okner found that *the richest 20 percent* of American families received *nearly half* (49.7 percent) of all the income received by families in 1966. This was considerably more than the amount received by the poorest 60 percent of American families, who received 29.7 percent of all family income. In crude terms, this means that while the wealthiest 40 million Americans had half the money pie to themselves, the least wealthy 120 million Americans had to share less than a third of that pie. At the extremes, the figures are even more outrageous. The top 1 percent of families received 10.5 percent of all income, which was three times as much as was received by the lowest 20 percent (who received 3.7 percent of income) and nearly as much was received by the lowest 40 percent of families (who received 13.6 percent of income). This means the wealthiest 1 percent of families—maybe 2 million souls—had nearly as much money to divide among themselves as the roughly 80 million persons who make up the bottom 40 percent. In a more recent essay, another Brookings economist, Arthur Okun, confirms the persistence of these disparities up to the present.[24]

The distribution of *wealth* (property such as stocks and land that generate income and tend to give one a say in major economic decisions) is even worse. An article in the November 1974 issue of *Survey of Current Business* reports that, in 1971,

> the *1 percent of U.S. families* (including single individuals) with the largest personal income accounted for *47 percent* of dividend income received and *51 percent* of the market value of stock owned by all families, while the *10 pecent of families* with the largest income accounted for *71 percent* of dividend income and *74 percent* of market value.[25]

I offer no complicated philosophical argument to prove that these disparities are unjust, although such arguments abound for those who are interested.[26] It is a scandal that in a nation as rich as ours, some 24 million people should live

below what the government conservatively defines as the
poverty level and that many millions more must scramble to
make ends meet. It is a scandal that in a nation as wealthy
as ours, so many millions cannot afford a proper diet, a college education, a decent place to live, and good health care.
We know too much about the causes of wealth and poverty to
believe that the rich become rich because of their talent or
contribution to society or that the poor are poor because they
are lazy or incapable. Since we are nowhere near offering all
Americans a good education and an equal opportunity to get
ahead, we have no right even to suggest that the distribution
of income reflects what people have truly earned. The distribution of income in America is so fundamentally shaped by
factors such as race, educational opportunity, and the economic class of one's parents[27] that few people who are well
off can honestly claim that they deserve all that they have.
Those who think they do should ask themselves where they
would be today if they had been born to migrant laborers in
California or to a poor black family in the Harlem ghetto.

   Enough said. I take it then as established that the disparities of wealth and income in America are wide and unjusti-
fied. For the vast majority—the many millions struggling to
make ends meet—to acquiesce in the vast wealth of a small
minority, it is necessary that the majority come to believe
that these disparities are justified, that the present order is
the best that human beings can accomplish, and that they
are not being ripped off by the have-plenties. In other words,
the system requires an effective ideology to fool enough of the
people enough of the time.

3.   The Willingness to Use Criminal Justice as Ideology

How does the discussion of ideology apply to criminal justice? I have discussed the unique visibility of criminal justice. I have discussed also the need for an ideology. If we add
to this the obvious fact that the criminal justice system is an
immensely powerful apparatus, uniquely empowered to use

force against American citizens, functioning at all levels of jurisdiction from the national FBI through state and city police to the smallest village's sheriff, and taking its shape and its orders from the holders of power in the United States, we should not be surprised to find the criminal justice system used to serve the interests of the powerful. And one way, although by no means the only way, of serving those interests is by performing the ideological function of legitimating the present order.

It is clear that the most powerful criminal justice policy-makers come from the have-plenties, not from the have-littles. This is most obvious in that the basic outlines of criminal justice policy are drawn by legislators, who make the criminal laws that define what is to be a subject of the criminal justice system in the first place, and by judges, who interpret those laws and define the limits of the powers of the police. It is no surprise that legislators and judges are pre-dominantly members of the the upper classes, if not at birth, then surely by the time they take office. One study of justices appointed to the U.S. Supreme Court between 1933 and 1957 found that 81 percent were sons of fathers with high social status occupations and that 61 percent had been educated in schools of high standing. Richard Quinney has compiled background data on key members of criminal justice policy-making and policy-advising committees and agencies, such as the President's Commission on Law Enforcement and Administration of Justice, the National Advisory Commis-sion on Civil Disorders, the National Commission on the Causes and Prevention of Violence, the Senate Judiciary Committee's Subcommittee on Criminal Laws and Proce-dures (the subcommittee had a strong hand in shaping the Omnibus Crime Control and Safe Streets Act of 1968), the Law Enforcement Assistance Administration, the Federal Bureau of Investigation, and last but not least the U.S. De-partment of Justice. With few exceptions, Quinney's report reads like a *Who's Who* of the business, legal, and political elite. For instance, 63 percent of the members of the Presi-dent's Crime Commission had business and corporate connections.[28]

If there is any doubt about the *willingness* of our leaders to use the criminal justice system for political aims, it should be noted that there is considerable evidence that the American criminal justice system has been used throughout its history in rather unsubtle ways to protect the interests of the powerful against the lower classes and political dissenters. The use of the FBI and local police forces to repress dissent by discrediting, harassing, and undermining dissident individuals and groups has been recently revealed. The FBI, often with active cooperation or tacit consent of local police, has engaged in literally hundreds of illegal burglaries of the offices of law-abiding left-wing political parties,[29] in political sabotage against the Black Panthers ("a Catholic priest, the Rev. Frank Curran, became the target of FBI operations because he permitted the Black Panthers to use his church for serving breakfasts to ghetto children"),[30] and in a campaign to discredit the late Martin Luther King, Jr. ("the FBI secretly categorized...King as a 'Communist' months before it ever started investigating him").[31] And although directors of the FBI have said that the bureau is "truly sorry" for these past abuses and that they are over, more recent reports indicate that they still continue.[32]

These acts of repression are only the latest in a long tradition. The first organized uniformed police force in the English-speaking world was established in London in 1829. They came to be called "bobbies" because of the role played by Sir Robert Peel in securing passage of the London Metropolitan Police Act which established the force. The first full-time uniformed police force in the United States was set up in New York City in 1845.[33] It was also in the period from the 1820s to the 1840s that the movement to build penitentiaries to house and reform criminals began in New York and Pennsylvania and spread rapidly through the states of the young nation.[34] That these are also the years that saw the beginnings of a large industrial working class in the cities of England and America is a coincidence too striking to ignore.

The police were repeatedly used to break strikes and harass strikers.[35] The penitentiaries were mainly used to house the laborers and foreigners (often one and the same) whom the middle and upper classes perceived as a threat.[36] Throughout the formative years of the American labor movement, public police forces, private police such as the Pinkertons, the National Guard, and regular army troops were repeatedly used to protect the interests of capital against the attempts of labor to organize in defense of its interests. The result was that "the United States has had the bloodiest and most violent labor history of any industrial nation in the world"—with most of the casualties on the side of labor.[37]

This much is enough to establish both the *need* for ideology and the *willingness* to use the criminal justice system to serve the interests of the powerful. The result is, I think, a plausible case for my claim that the criminal justice system is allowed to function (or dysfunction) in the particular way it does because this performs an ideological service that protects the interests of the powerful.

* * *

At this point the Defender of the Present Legal Order enters with an objection that may have troubled you. An avid TV viewer, the defender states with authority that TV crime shows do not always or even most often portray poor people as criminals. Very often the criminals are wealthy business executives or socialites or the higher-ups in organized crime who affect the life-style of the upper classes. So, the Defender maintains, if there is any "message" at all from the media, it is that crime is the work of people from all economic classes.

I think the Defender is missing the forest for the trees. It is quite true that TV villains are drawn rather equitably from all classes of society. Undoubtedly, this is at least partly the result of the fact that the more intricate crimes of the well-to-do in business or organized crime make more interesting hatching and catching and thus more interesting watching than the rather mundane muggings and small-time holdups of the poor—certainly if you have to generate 133 plots a week. But what remains constant, even as the economic class

of the TV criminal goes up and down, is the *kind* of crime he
or she commits. Regardless of how affluent TV villains are,
they are almost invariably portrayed as committing an FBI
Index Crime—what I have characterized as a *one-on-one
harm*, the Typical Crime. That is, no matter how much
money is in their pockets, the TV crook commits a more or
less complicated version of the *kinds of crimes for which
poor people are mainly arrested, convicted, and sentenced in
the real world:* murder, assault, or theft. In fact, when a TV
show does unearth an upper-class crime such as blackmail or
embezzlement, it is usually *as a motive for* murder or theft.
So, regardless of who the TV producers portray as a criminal,
the *image of crime* offered the viewer is the image of the kinds
of crime committed by the poor in real life. And this, in conjunction with news reports on who really gets arrested and
who really is in prison, is enough to carry the ideological message that real crimes are the work of the poor.

In fact, one might go further and speculate that the present
TV crime fare is the best way of getting across the very message that I spelled out in section b above. Television's "equitable" portrayal of both the rich and the poor as committing
what are basically the crimes of the poor, in more or less complicated form, may serve the *ideological* function in the most
effective way. Think of what it conveys.

First, it conveys the message that there are no dangerous
crimes unique to the wealthy—such as price-fixing or tolerat-
ing occupational hazards—and so it confirms the bias we
have already seen to be built into the very definition of serious crime. *Second,* it conveys the message that the criminal
justice system pursues rich and poor alike, so that when it
happens mainly to pounce on the poor in real life, it is not
out of any class bias. It is simply doing justice. *Third,* it
conveys the message that crime is not the result of the deprivations of poverty but rather of individual moral failings,
such as greed, that are equitably distributed to members of
all economic classes. The result of this is that when the poor
do get arrested and punished for crimes in real life, the rest of
us do not have to believe that poverty *caused* their crime but

that it was caused by their own moral failings and thus they are just getting what they deserve.[38]

In other words, the result of this is that the system can produce an identification of crime and poverty without producing sympathy for the criminal! And this is, as we have seen, the message conveyed by the criminal justice system in real life. One can hardly think of a better example of having one's cake and eating it. This amounts to a plausible case that the TV portrayal of crime could not serve the wealthy better if they tried. And this, in turn, should be considered in light of the fact that as of fall 1976, prime-time TV commercial time is selling at an average of $90,000 a minute![39] At prices like that, it is not hard to believe that the wealthy corporations that buy TV time are going to pay for the kinds of programs that serve them best.[40]

d. Gathering Up the Fruits of Pyrrhic Defeat

To summarize, let us quickly retrace the ground we have covered in order to put the arguments in perspective and exhibit the capacity of the Pyrrhic defeat theory to make criminal justice policy and practice intelligible.

In Chapter 1, we saw that the criminal justice system is failing to reduce crime and that this failure is, at least to a considerable degree, avoidable. It is not so much our inability to stem the rising tide of crime that calls for explanation but rather our unwillingness to reduce crime that must be explained.

In response to this, I offered the Pyrrhic defeat theory of the failure of criminal justice. As its name suggests, this is the view that there are sufficient profits from defeat in the war on crime to transform it into victory for those with the power to make criminal justice policy.

To understand these profits, we had to understand that criminal justice is not just failing but is failing while making it look like crime is a threat from the poor. In other words, it is refusing to reduce the *real* threat of crime while conveying the *image* that crime is the work of the poor. In Chapters 2 and 3, we saw how the criminal justice system reacts not simply to the dangers that threaten society but primarily to the dangers threatened by poor folks. This is compounded by a systemwide bias that ensures that our prisons will be predominantly filled with the poor, thus giving living testimony to the fact that the really dangerous people in our society are poor people. Why else would we lock them up like animals?

In Chapter 4, I described the profits of this combination of failing to reduce crime and making it look like the poor are the really dangerous people in our society. These profits lie in the ideological message conveyed by the criminal justice system's biased failure. The message is two-pronged:

1. By focusing on *individual* criminals, the criminal justice system diverts attention away from the irrationalities and injustices of our social and economic institutions.
2. By focusing on *poor* criminals, the criminal justice system diverts attention away from the rich and powerful who most profit from our social and economic institutions. And the *failure* to reduce crime at all reinforces this by diverting fear and hostility on to the poor.

The sum total of this is to divert attention both from the injustices of the social order and from those who occupy positions of power and privilege in that order. Since these are the very people that could change criminal justice policy if they were so inclined, we have an explanation for why the system is allowed to fail in the way it does. For them, *nothing succeeds like failure.*

For them, the fruits of Pyrrhic defeat in the war on crime transform defeat into victory. The fruits of this Pyrrhic defeat are purchased not merely with the tax dollars of the mass of Americans, not merely with the freedom of those who are imprisoned not because they are guilty but because they are guilty and poor, but with the bodies of those Americans who would be spared injury and death if our criminal justice system were really aimed at protecting society from

those who most genuinely threaten it. In the next chapter, we
will consider the moral implications of this purchase.

Footnotes

1. *Challenge*, p. 44.
2. Answering a question like this poses the most difficult prob-
    lems for social theory. Absolute confirmation would require
    that we be able to read the minds of policymakers and perhaps
    even penetrate into the realm of their subconscious wishes.
    Even this might not suffice, since the purposes that guide
    large and complex social institutions may be unknown to their
    members. For instance, it is sometimes argued that the "pur-
    pose" of funeral rites is to reaffirm community values by
    solemnly and exaggeratedly eulogizing the departed before his
    or her assembled survivors. It is sometimes argued that
    hierarchy among humans and animals serves the purpose of
    preventing competition that could degenerate into destructive
    warfare. And, of course, we have already encountered the sug-
    gestion of Erikson and Durkheim that crime or deviance draws
    the community closer together. In each of these cases, a
    social institution has a purpose beyond the knowledge of its
    participants. It functions simply because the realization of
    this purpose provides satisfactions even when the participants
    are unaware that they have been pursuing it. It is in precisely
    these terms that I shall try to answer the question why the
    criminal justice system is allowed to fail in the way it does.
    I shall argue that whether or not the policymakers consciously
    intend it, the "failure" of criminal justice serves a purpose
    that provides satisfactions for them even if they are unaware
    of pursuing it. Necessarily this argument is the most specula-
    tive and most difficult to prove in the whole book. It should be
    noted that while it completes and draws together the argu-
    ments in the first three chapters, the truth of those arguments
    is independent of the truth of this one. Regardless of whether
    you accept my answer to the question of *why*, it remains true
    that the system is failing inexcusably and that it is biased
    against the poor in a degree that is an outrage against justice.
3. For whites earning between $15,000 and $25,000 a year, there
    are 94 cases of robbery with serious assault per 100,000; for

whites earning over $25,000, the incidence of robbery with serious assault is 12 per 100,000. On the other hand, for every 100,000 whites earning under $3000 a year, 199 are victims of robbery with serious assault—and for nonwhites in the same boat financially the victimization rate is 302 per 100,000. The incidence of aggravated assault with injury is 221 for every 100,000 white persons earning between $15,000 and $25,000, and 142 for every 100,000 whites earning over $25,000. For whites earning under $3000 a year, the rate of aggravated assaults with injury is 531, and for nonwhites with the same income, 1060 for every 100,000 individuals. *Sourcebook*, p. 236.

4. A report to the Federal Communications Commission estimates that by the time the average American child reaches age 14, he or she has seen 13,000 human beings killed by violence on television. Although a few of these are probably killed by science fiction monsters, the figure still suggests that the extent of the impact of the televised portrayal of crime and the struggle against it, on the imaginations of Americans, is nothing short of astounding. See Eve Merriam, "We're Teaching Our Children that Violence Is Fun," in *Violence: An Element of American Life*, eds., K. Taylor and F. Soady, Jr. (Boston: Holbrook Press, 1972), p. 155. For a list of the 20 police programs (which does not include detective programs and other shows in which the fight against crime is the theme) aired on ABC, CBS, and NBC, the three major networks, see Center for Research on Criminal Justice, *The Iron Fist and the Velvet Glove: An Analysis of the U.S. Police*, pp. 194-195.

5. Richard A. Cloward and Lloyd E. Ohlin, *Delinquency and Opportunity: A Theory of Delinquent Gangs* (New York: The Free Press, 1960), esp. pp. 77-107.

6. Ibid., p. 81.

7. Ibid., p. 105.

8. Ibid., p. 107.

9. Ibid., p. 105.

10. Willem Bonger, *Criminality and Economic Conditions*, abridged and with an introduction by Austin T. Turk (Bloomington, Indiana: Indiana University Press, 1969), pp. 7-12, 40-47. Willem Adriaan Bonger was born in Holland in 1876 and died by his own hand in 1940 rather than submit to the Nazis. His *Criminalité et conditions économiques* first appeared in 1905. It was translated into English and published in the United States in 1916. Ibid., pp. 3-4.

11. David M. Gordon, "Capitalism, Class and Crime in America," *Crime and Delinquency* (April 1973), p. 174.
12. Ibid., p. 174.
13. William and Mary Morris, *Dictionary of Word and Phrase Origins*, II (New York: Harper and Row, 1967), p. 282.
14. *Sourcebook*, pp. 203, 204, 223, 207; see also p. 177.
15. Historical documentation of this can be found in David J. Rothman, *The Discovery of the Asylum: Social Order and Disorder in the New Republic* (Boston: Little, Brown, 1971); and in Frances Fox Piven and Richard A. Cloward, *Regulating the Poor: The Functions of Public Welfare* (New York: Pantheon, 1971), which carries the analysis up to the present.
16. *The Republic of Plato*, trans. F. M. Cornford (New York: Oxford University Press, 1945), p. 18 [I. 338]. Plato was born in Athens in the year 428 B.C. (or 427, depending on the reckoning) and died there in 348 B.C. (or 347). Scholars generally agree that at least Book One of *The Republic* (the section in which Thrasymachus speaks) was written between the death of Socrates in 399 B.C. and Plato's first journey to Sicily, from which he returned in 388 B.C. (or 387). See Frederick Copleston, S. J., *A History of Philosophy, Volume I: Greece and Rome* Westminster, Maryland: The Newman Press, 1946), pp. 127-141.
17. Karl Marx and Friedrich Engels, *Manifesto of the Communist Party*, in *The Marx-Engels Reader*, ed., Robert C. Tucker (New York: W. W. Norton, 1972), p. 337. Marx was born in Trier, Prussia (now in West Germany) on May 5, 1818, and died on March 14, 1883. The *Manifesto* was first published in London in February, 1848—when Marx was nearly 30 years old. Ibid., pp. xi-xiv.
18. A recent article on congressional ethics in *Newsweek* (June 14, 1976) makes the point so graphically that it is worth quoting at length:

> ...Some of the Hill's most powerful veterans have long earned part of their income from outside business interests—and may be tempted to vote with their own bank accounts in mind when legislation affecting those interests has come before Congress. House whip Thomas P. (Tip) O'Neill is active in real estate and insurance in Massachusetts, Minority Leader John Rhodes of Arizona is a director and vice-president of a life insurance company

and scores of other senior members are involved with the banking industry, oil and gas companies and farming operations. Do these connections destroy their judgment? Not necessarily, argues Russell Long of Louisiana, chairman of the powerful Senate Finance Committee and a reliable defender of oil interests—who nevertheless refuses to disclose the size of his personal oil and gas holdings, most of them inherited from his father, former Gov. Huey Long. "A long time ago I became convinced that if you have financial interests completely parallel to your state, then you have no problem," says Long. "If I didn't represent the oil and gas industry, I wouldn't represent the state of Louisiana."

Even more difficult to trace is the influence of representatives who keep their law practices— and their clients, many of whom do business with the Federal government—when they become members of Congress. [p. 25]

See Richard Quinney, *Critique of Legal Order: Crime Control in Capitalist Society* (Boston: Little, Brown, 1973), pp. 82-84, for an account of the financial interests and corporate connections of the members of the influential Committee for Economic Development—the domestic policy counterpart of the Council on Foreign Relations. For similar information on the members of various committees and councils that shape American foreign policy, see G. William Domhoff, "Who Made American Foreign Policy, 1945-1963?," in *Corporations and the Cold War*, ed., David Horowitz (New York: Monthly Review Press, 1969), pp. 25-69.

19. Marx, *The German Ideology*, in *The Marx-Engels Reader*, ed., Tucker, p. 136.

20. Each new ruling class "is compelled, merely in order to carry through its aim, to represent its interest as the common interest of all the members of society," Marx, *The German Ideology*, in *The Marx-Engels Reader*, ed., Tucker, p. 138.

21. Marx was not the first to use the term "ideology." The term was coined by Antoine Destutt de Tracy, who was among the intellectuals named in 1795 to direct the researches of the newly founded Institut de France. The *idéologues* of the Institut generally believed that existing ideas were prejudices rooted in individual psychology or in political conditions and that the path to liberation from these prejudices and thus toward a

rational society lay in a science of ideas (literally, an "idea-ology") which made human beings aware of the sources of their ideas. Thomas Jefferson introduced the theory of ideology in America. He tried (albeit unsuccessfully) to have Destutt de Tracy's theory made part of the original curriculum of the University of Virginia. See George Lichtheim, "The Concept of Ideology," *History and Theory,* 4, No. 2 (1965), pp. 164-195; and *Ideology, Politics, and Political Theory,* ed., Richard H. Cox (Belmont, California: Wadsworth, 1969), pp. 7-8. Needless to say, Marx used the term "ideology" in ways that neither Destutt de Tracy nor Jefferson anticipated.

22. Lichtheim's essay provides a good discussion of the philosophical antecedents of the gradual separation of the notion of *ideology* from that of *false consciousness.* Undoubtedly, this separation is of a piece with the current wisdom that takes it as the height of brilliance to point out that all views of the world are conditioned and rendered partial by the limits of the viewer's historical and social vantage point and thus shrinks from trying to say anything *true* about the human condition. An illuminating contemporary example of this "current wisdom" applied to the criminal justice system is Walter B. Miller, "Ideology and Criminal Justice Policy: Some Current Issues," *Journal of Criminal Law and Criminology,* 64, No. 2 (1973), pp. 141-162. I shall use the concept of ideology in the Marxian sense, that is, to include that of false consciousness.

23. What follows is just a smattering of the literature documenting either the wide and abiding disparities of wealth in America or the existence of a very small, not necessarily organized, group of individuals who, in addition to being extremely wealthy, make most of the economic and political decisions that shape America's destiny: G. William Domhoff, *Who Rules America?* (Englewood Cliffs, N.J.: Prentice-Hall, 1967); Richard C. Edwards, Michael Reich, and Thomas E. Weisskopf, *The Capitalist System: A Radical Analysis of American Society* (Englewood Cliffs, N.J.: Prentice-Hall, 1972); John Kenneth Galbraith, *The New Industrial State* (New York: Signet Books, 1968); Edward S. Greenberg, *Serving the Few: Corporate Capitalism and the Bias of Government Policy* (New York: John Wiley, 1974); Gabriel Kolko, *Wealth and Power in America: An Analysis of Social Class and Income Distribution* New York: Praeger, 1962); C. Wright Mills, *The Power Elite* (New York: Oxford University Press, 1956); Joseph A. Pech-

man and Benjamin A. Okner, *Who Bears the Tax Burden?*
(Washington, D.C.: The Brookings Institution, 1974); Philip M.
Stern, *The Rape of the Taxpayer* (New York: Vintage Books,
1974).

24. The statistics are from Pechman and Okner, p. 46. Their figures for family income are adjusted to account for underreporting and nonreporting of items like accrued capital gains,
imputed rent, and the like, which are often not figured in
money income but which do enhance purchasing power. Ibid.,
pp. 19, 45. See also Arthur M. Okun, *Equality and Efficiency:
The Big Tradeoff* (Washington, D.C: The Brookings Institution, 1975), pp. 65-82. Okun's figures differ somewhat from
those of Pechman and Okner, but his conclusions are basically
the same. Gabriel Kolko has argued that contrary to prevailing mythology, these disparities have remained relatively
stable throughout the twentieth century. In 1910, the richest
20 percent received 46.2 percent of personal income, and the
poorest 20 percent received 8.3 percent. In 1959, the richest 20
percent received 44.7 percent of personal income and the poorest 20 percent received 4.0 percent (Kolko, p. 14). Not a very
impressive track record for the land of opportunity. Pechman
continues the analysis up through 1967 and points out that not
only has the share of the richest 20 percent remained relatively unchanged in the time from 1952 to 1967 but that taxes
have relatively no impact on this distribution. The top 15 percent of the population held 36 percent of income *before* taxes
and 34 percent *after* taxes. So much for the redistributive effect
of our so-called progressive income tax. Joseph Pechman,
"The Rich, the Poor, and the Taxes They Pay," *The Public
Interest*, No. 17 (Fall, 1969), pp. 23, 24, 28, inter alia. Pechman
points out that what progressivity there is in the federal income tax is more than offset by the Social Security payroll
tax and state and local taxes, all of which are regressive in
effect. Ibid., pp. 26-33. (A tax is progressive if the tax rate—
percentage of income to be paid to the government—increases
as one's income increases. A tax is regressive if the percentage
paid out in taxes increases as one's income gets lower.) Elsewhere, Pechman and Okner have pointed out that even though
marginal tax rates for federal income tax range from 14 to 70
percent, a variety of loopholes are available that have the effect of making the maximum effective tax rate 32 percent, and
"the average effective rate does not exceed 25 pecent until in-

come levels of $100,000 and over." Joseph Pechman and Benjamin Okner, *Individual Income Tax Erosion by Income Classes*, Reprint 230 (Washington, D.C.: Brookings Institution, 1972), p. 21.

25. Marshall E. Blume, Jean Crockett, and Irwin Friend, "Stockownership in the United States: Characteristics and Trends," *Survey of Current Business*, 54, No. 11 (November, 1974), p. 17. (Emphasis added.)

26. Undoubtedly, the most interesting recent work on this topic is John Rawls's *A Theory of Justice* (Cambridge, Mass.: Harvard University Press, 1971). The noted British philosopher Stuart Hampshire has called it the most important work in moral philosophy since the Second World War. It is sure to exert considerable influence on theoretical discussions of political, legal, and economic justice. Rawls's approach is essentially "naturalistic." That is, he takes the "good" to be that which people rationally desire, and the "moral good" to be that which would best serve *all* people's rational desires. Based on this, he takes justice to be those social (legal, political, economic, etc.) arrangements that best serve the interests of all. To reach specific principles of justice, he asks for those principles that it would be rational for all people to agree to if each could not use force or influence to tailor the principles to his or her own interest. On the question of the distribution of income or wealth, this way of questioning leads to the principle that economic inequalities are only just if they work to everyone's advantage, for instance, as incentives that work to raise the level of productivity and thus the level of well-being for all. It would be the task of government to rectify inequalities that exceed this point, by means of taxes and transfers. I cannot, of course, do justice here to what Rawls takes 600 pages to explain and defend. However, I offer this short summary to suggest that the disparities of income in America are far from just in the light of contemporary moral philosophy. Clearly, those disparities are far greater than anything that could be claimed to be *necessary* to increase the well-being of all. Indeed, one would have to be blind not to see that they are not increasing the well-being of all. Robert Nozick has replied to Rawls in a book entitled *Anarchy, State and Utopia* (New York: Basic Books, 1974), which no doubt represents the free enterprise system's theory of justice. Nozick holds that no theory (such as Rawls's) that calls for government intervention to rectify income distribu-

tion can be just. His argument is that if people acquire their property (including money) legitimately, then they have the right to spend or sell it as they wish. If this leads to disparities in wealth, one cannot alter this outcome without denying that those spenders or sellers had the right to dispose of their property or money as they saw fit. I shall not try to answer Nozick here. It should be noted, however, that his view starts from the assumption that the property or money that is sold or spent was acquired legitimately. In light of the fact that so much American property was stolen at gunpoint from Indians or Mexicans and so much wealth taken from the hides of black slaves, it is questionable whether Nozick's theory can be applied in the American context. It might require a redistribution of wealth just so that we could reach the starting point at which we could say that individuals own what they own legitimately.

27. One study reports that "among high school graduates with *equal* academic ability, the proportion going on to college averages nearly 25 percentage points lower for males (and nearly 35 for females) in the bottom socioeconomic quarter of the population than in the top quarter." And another indicates that "the sons of families in the top fifth of the socioeconomic pyramid have average incomes 75 percent higher than those coming from the bottom fifth." Okun, *Equality and Efficiency*, p. 81 and p. 75.

28. J. A. Schmidhauser, "The Justices of the Supreme Court: A Collective Portrait," *Midwest Journal of Political Science* 3 (1959), pp. 2-37, 40-49, cited in William J. Chambliss and Robert B. Seidman, *Law, Order, and Power* (Reading, Mass.: Addison-Wesley, 1971), p. 96; and Richard Quinney, *Critique of Legal Order: Crime Control in Capitalist Society* (Boston: Little, Brown, 1973), pp. 60-82, 86-92.

29. "F.B.I. Burglarized Leftist Offices Here 92 Times in 1960-66, Official Files Show," *The New York Times*, March 29, 1976, p. 1; "Burglaries by FBI Listed in Hundreds." *The Washington Post*, July 16, 1975, p. 1. See also *Cointelpro: The FBI's Secret War on Political Freedom*, ed., Cathy Perkus, introduction by Noam Chomsky (New York: Monad Press, 1975).

30. "Hill Panel Raps FBI's Anti-Panthers Tactics," *The Washington Post*, May 7, 1976, pp. A1, A22.

31. "FBI Labeled King 'Communist' in '62," *The Washington Post*, May 6, 1976, pp. A1, A26.

32. "Kelley Says FBI Is 'Truly Sorry' for Past Abuses," *The Washington Post*, May 9, 1976, pp. A1, A14; "FBI Break-ins Still Go On, Panel Reports," *The Washington Post*, May 11, 1976, pp. A1, A16; and "The FBI: Bag Jobs," *Newsweek*, July 4, 1976, pp. 84-85.

33. James F. Richardson, *Urban Police in the United States* (Port Washington, N.Y.: Kennikat Press, 1974), pp. 8-13, 22. See also Richardon's *The New York Police: Colonial Times to 1901* (New York: Oxford University Press, 1970).

34. Rothman, *The Discovery of the Asylum*, pp. 57-108, esp. 79-81. Cf. Michel Foucault, *Discipline and Punish: The Birth of the Prison* (London: Allen Lane, 1977).

35. Richardson, *Urban Police*, pp. 158-161. See also R. Boyer and H. Morais, *Labor's Untold Story* (New York: United Electrical, Radio & Machine Workers of America, 1976).

36. Rothman, pp. 253-254.

37. Philip Taft and Philip Ross, "American Labor Violence: Its Causes, Character, and Outcome," in *The History of Violence in America*, eds., H. D. Graham and T. R. Gurr (New York: Bantam, 1969), pp. 281-395, esp. pp. 281, 380; and Richard E. Rubenstein, *Rebels in Eden: Mass Political Violence in the United States* (Boston: Little, Brown, 1970), p. 81, inter alia. See also Center for Research in Criminal Justice, *The Iron Fist and the Velvet Glove* (Berkeley, California, 1975), pp. 16-19.

38. In fact, although people tend to think of crime as the work of the poor, very few people think that poverty *causes* crime. A Gallup poll conducted in 1972 found only 13 percent of those interviewed named poverty or unemployment as a cause of the high crime rate in the U.S. *Sourcebook*, p. 177.

39. *TV Guide* (Washington-Baltimore Edition), June 26-July 2 (1976), p. A1.

40. One study of television viewers, found that heavy viewers (four or more hours a day) perceive the world to be more violent and dangerous than it really is and than it is perceived by light viewers (two or less hours a day). The authors suggest that this may have the effect of increasing the demand for, and the legitimacy of, established authority. They conclude:

> Throughout history, once a ruling class has established its rule, the primary function of its cultural media has been the legitimization and maintenance of its authority....

We have found that violence on prime-time network TV cultivates exaggerated assumptions about the threat of danger in the real world. Fear is a universal emotion, and easy to exploit. The exaggerated sense of risk and insecurity may lead to increasing demands for protection, and to increasing pressure for the use of force by the established authority.

George Gerbner and Larry Gross, "The Scary World of TV's Heavy Viewer," *Psychology Today*, 9, No. 11 (April 1976), pp. 41-45, 89.

5

Criminal *Justice* or *Criminal* Justice: A Matter of Moral Conviction

What are states without justice but robber-bands enlarged?

St. Augustine, *Confessions*

. . . unjust social arrangements are themselves a kind of extortion, even violence. . . .

John Rawls, *A Theory of Justice*

. . . the policeman . . . moves through Harlem, therefore, like an occupying soldier in a bitterly hostile country; which is precisely what, and where he is, and is the reason he walks in twos and threes.

James Baldwin, *Nobody Knows My Name*

a. The Crime of Justice

Robbers, extortionists, occupying soldiers—these are the
terms used to characterize those who enforce an unjust law
and an unjust order. It would be a mistake to think that this
is merely a matter of rhetoric. There is a very real and very
important sense in which those who use force unjustly or
who use force to protect an unjust social order are no different
from a band of criminals or an occupying army. In this
chapter, I want to prove that this is true.

Without this proof, you are likely to think that what has
been described in the first three chapters and accounted for
in the fourth amounts to no more than another call for reform
of the criminal justice system to make it more effective and
more fair, when in fact it is much more. What I want to argue
is that a criminal justice system that functions like ours, one
that imposes its penalties on the poor and not equally on all
who threaten society, one that does not protect us against
threats to our lives and possessions equal to or graver than
those presently defined as "crimes," and one that fails even
to do those things that could better protect us against the
crimes of the poor is a criminal justice system that *is morally
no better than the criminality it claims to fight.*

At the end of this chapter, I propose some reforms of the
system. However, these should not be taken as proposals
aimed merely at improving the effectiveness or fairness of
American criminal justice. If the argument of this chapter is
correct, then these proposals represent the necessary conditions for establishing the moral superiority of criminal
justice to criminality. They are the conditions that must be
fulfilled if the criminal justice system is to be acquitted of the
indictment implicit in the statements of Baldwin, Rawls, and
St. Augustine.

Since the argument that follows is of central importance to
the very meaning of the criticisms already presented and to
the urgency of the reforms proposed, the argument will be set
forth in dialogue form, since this is the form closest to the
way we argue among (and within) ourselves and thus is most

accessible and most easily understood. Further, I assume that there are those among you who may be willing to believe the criticisms thus far presented but are reluctant to accept the more profound indictment to which these criticisms amount. By using the dialogue form, I can hope to anticipate and respond to such objections.

Before beginning, a word of introduction is in order to sketch out the terrain in which the dialogue will take place and to give you an idea of the route that will be followed in traversing that terrain.

What is common to the charge implicit in the statements of Baldwin, Rawls and St. Augustine is the idea that *injustice transforms a legal system into its opposite.* What is common to the robber, the extortionist, and the occupying soldier is that each uses force (or the threat of force) to coerce other people to do things against their own interests. The robber and the extortionist use force to make other people hand over things of value. The occupying soldier uses force to subject one people to domination by another.

A legal system, of course, also uses force. But its defenders maintain that it uses force to protect people's control over the things they value and over their own destinies. That is, they claim that the legal system protects what people possess against robbers and extortionists and protects their autonomy against anyone who would try to impose their will on them by force. In short, although both a legal system and its opposite—either criminality or military domination—use force, the moral superiority of the legal system lies in the fact that it uses force to secure the interests of the very people subject to its force, while criminals and occupation troops use force to subject some people to the interests of others.

The moral legitimacy of a legal system and the lack of legitimacy of crime and military domination hinge, then, on the question of whether or not coercion is being used to enhance people's own interests. Ordinarily, when anyone is forced to serve as an instrument for the purposes of others, we call this tyranny or exploitation—or, in a word, *injustice.* In the absence of some compelling moral reason, force used to coerce people into serving the interests of others at the expense of their own is *morally no better than criminal force*. Since a legal system purports to do the reverse—to use force to protect *everyone's* interest in freedom and security by preventing and rectifying violations of those interests by others—legal systems call themselves *systems of justice*.[1] With this, they assert that the force used under color of law is morally opposite from, and morally superior to, the force used by criminals or conquerors.

This adds up to something that should be obvious but is not. *A criminal justice system is criminal to the extent that it is not a system of justice.* And the requirements of justice are the familiar ones. The system must truly protect everyone's interests, not the interests of some more than others. And it must use its force against everyone who endangers those interests, but not against some more than others. In sum, a criminal justice system is a system of justice to the extent that it protects equally the interests and rights of all and to the extent that it punishes equally all who endanger these interests or violate these rights. To the extent that it veers from this, the criminal justice system is guilty of the same sacrificing of the interests of some for the benefit of others that it exists to combat. It is therefore, morally speaking, guilty of crime.

The experience of the twentieth century has taught us that we should not take for granted that every legal system is a system of justice. Hitler's Germany and Stalin's Russia, as well as contemporary South Africa, are testimony to the fact that what is put forth as law may well be outrageously unjust. That is, we have come to recognize that truth implicit in the statements of Baldwin, Rawls, and St. Augustine: that what is put forth under color of law may be morally no better than crime or tyranny. Once we recognize this, we can no longer uncritically take for granted that our own legal order is just merely because it is legal. We must subject it to the moral test of whether it serves and protects the interests of all to make sure that it is not injustice disguised as justice, criminality wearing the mask of law.

It is, of course, not my aim to place the American legal system on par with that of Hitler's Germany or Stalin's Russia. As I have acknowledged more than once already, there is much in the system that is legitimate and many are caught by the system who should be. Rather my claim is this:

- *To the extent that* the American criminal justice system *fails* to implement policies that could significantly reduce crime and the suffering it produces (as argued in Chapter 1),
- *To the extent that* the American criminal justice system *fails* to protect Americans against the gravest dangers to their lives and property (as argued in Chapter 2),
- *To the extent that* the American criminal justice system apprehends and punishes individuals, not because they are dangerous, but because they are *dangerous and poor* (as argued in Chapter 3),
- *Then, to that same extent,* the American criminal justice system fails to give Americans either protection or justice and aids and abets those who pose the greatest dangers to Americans and *thus its use of force is morally no better than crime itself.*

Let us now join the dialogue between the Critic and the Defender of the Present Legal Order. By now neither of them needs any introduction.

Defender: See here, Critic, I've been listening quite patiently to you and I'm willing to agree to much of what you've said so far, but now I think you are letting your emotions get the best of you. I admit that our criminal justice system is far from perfect. I admit it may even be in need of a major overhaul. But to call it *criminal* is either just rhetoric or—if you mean it literally—confusion. A crime is a violation of the law. A legal system may be unjust, but to call it "criminal" is to ask for confusion, since a legal system can't violate the law—it is the law!

Critic: How foolish do you think I am? Surely you don't take me to be saying that the legal system is criminal in the sense of breaking the law.

Defender: Then say what you mean. If I'm confused, it's because your argument asks for confusion.

Critic: Maybe so. Then let me try again. My point is that if what I've said about the system is true. . . . You grant that what I have said in the first three chapters is true, don't you?

Defender: Yes, yes. I already said I did. Get on with it.

Critic: Well, then, if that's true, I hold that it means that the criminal justice system is *morally indistinguishable from criminality*. That is, its use of force is morally wrong for the same reasons that make the criminal's use of force morally wrong. And what is morally indistinguishable from criminality *is* essentially criminal in every respect other than the technical one of being a violation of the criminal law.

Defender: A mere technicality, is it? I suppose I'm splitting hairs to point out that a crime is a violation of the law.

Critic: You're not splitting hairs, but you are missing an important point. Crime is morally wrong because it uses force in ways that hurt people without moral justification and because it uses the threat of force to make people do what they might not otherwise freely choose to do. Now the criminal justice system also uses force in ways that hurt people. . . .

Defender: You mean the use of force to arrest suspects or to confine convicts?

Critic: Yes. But also it uses the threat of force to limit the freedom of just about everyone else.

Defender: Here I take it that you are referring to the fact that the system threatens punishment as a way of forcing people to comply with the criminal law.

Critic: Right again. And this means not only complying with law but putting up with the social and economic arrangements that the law protects. Just as the criminal law limits the ways in which homosexuals express their sexual desires, so it limits the ways in which the poor can alleviate the miseries of poverty or the powerless can gain more control over their lives. For instance, we've seen that the system allows harmful business practices such as pollution and inadequate occupational safety to exist. Now if the victims of these practices took action in their own self-defense against these practices, they would come up against the very property rights that the criminal justice system protects. But this means that by enforcing laws against theft and assault and the rest, *the criminal justice system is using force in ways that protect those harmful practices.* All of which means that a criminal justice system uses force in ways that directly produce considerable suffering—for example, the suffering of those who languish in prison cages or of those who must seriously limit their free expression in fear of languishing in prison—and it uses force in ways that indirectly produce considerable suffering—for example, the suffering of those who receive the short end of the stick in the economic system, which the criminal justice system protects with force and the threat of force.

Defender: What you're saying is obvious. Get to the point.

Critic: Yes, of course. The point is obvious also. Both crime and criminal justice use force and the threat of force in ways that directly and indirectly lead to human suffering. If there is a difference, it must be a *moral* difference.

Defender: Not a *legal* difference? Isn't it enough that the criminal's use of force is against the law and the criminal justice system's use of force is legal?

Critic: That's not enough, because the question we are asking is: What makes the use of force under color of law morally superior to the use of force outside the law? And enough evil has been perpetrated in the name of law to prove

that a legal difference is not enough. Do you think that
Hitler's actions were not criminal just because they were
allowed by Nazi law?

Defender: No.

Critic: Then we must ask what the moral justification is
that makes the criminal justice system's use of force superior
to the criminal's?

Defender: But the answer is obvious. What the enforcers
of law do is morally right because it is necessary to protect
society. You do believe there is a right of self-defense, don't
you.

Critic: Yes, of course.

Defender: You do believe that the right to self-defense is a
moral justification for the use of force, even deadly force, in
one's defense, don't you?

Critic: Yes, again.

Defender: Well, that's enough. A criminal justice system
is a society's form of self-defense. Since those who attack it
use force, sometimes deadly force, the society has the right to
use that much force in its defense—and it does this through
the criminal justice system domestically, just as it does it
through the military internationally.

Critic: Don't leave justice out of the picture.

Defender: Certainly, self-defense is neither the sole goal
nor the sole justification for the system. The system is also
justified in using force to do justice—to punish the evildoer
and so forth. And this is compatible with the goal of self-
defense, since if other potential criminals see that actual
criminals receive their just deserts, then hopefully they'll
think twice about crime.

Critic: But sometimes the goal of justice seems to go
against that of society's self-defense, doesn't it? For example,
when a person is acquitted by reason of insanity we are

hardly made safer. Nor are we made safer when an otherwise guilty person is released because the evidence that would convict him was the result of an illegal search.

Defender: I think these are some of the finest aspects of our system. They prove that we are willing to accept some risks rather than punish those who are not responsible for their acts or convict someone unfairly—even if he or she did commit a crime. I admit there is some tension between the goals of justice and self-defense, just as there is tension in an individual between the goals of freedom and security or between the ideals of integrity and satisfaction. But you and I don't have to resolve this tension. All I want to maintain is that what the criminal justice system does is morally superior to what criminals do, because it is done in the name of the ideals of justice and self-defense.

Critic: Thanks.

Defender: Thanks for what?

Critic: For proving my point.

Defender: Proving your . . . ?

Critic: I agree that the moral credentials of criminal justice are to be found in the moral goals of justice and protection of society. Indeed, I would argue that a criminal justice system really aimed at achieving justice and protecting society would be using force to promote *everyone's* interests—and that would make it clearly superior to crime or conquest which use force to promote particular interests. But my whole argument so far is that one can barely comprehend criminal justice policy if one looks at it as aimed at justice and the protection of society. After all, it refuses to make changes that might reduce what are now labeled serious crimes—those on the FBI Index. It refuses to treat as crimes acts that are at least as dangerous to society as these. And others that it does label crimes, such as the illegal machinations of corporate executives, it treats delicately, if at all. So much for protecting society. As for justice, the system punishes some people for acts that are not at all harmful such as homosexuality or prostitution or smoking marijuana, and allows others who gravely endanger society to go unpunished. And then, of course, the fact that criminals are mainly punished, not because they are criminals, but because they are *poor* criminals is itself a howling injustice. The system does not use force in everyone's interest: it imposes force disproportionately upon the poor while leaving society vulnerable to the harmful acts of the well-off. So if the moral difference between the criminal's use of force and the criminal justice system's use of force lies in justice and self-defense— as you have so eloquently argued—my point is made.

Defender: While you were just holding forth, it occurred to me what's been bothering me about your argument. Your mistake finally dawned on me.

Critic: Well please tell me what it is. If I am mistaken, I'll gladly revise my views. I get no pleasure from thinking that the criminal *justice* system is a *criminal* justice system.

Defender: You admitted earlier that you accept that most if not all the people who end up in prison are probably guilty of the crime or crimes that got them there.

Critic: It's hard to know these things with certainty, but I start from the assumption that those people did commit the acts that they were sentenced for and that they are *legally* guilty of those crimes. So?

Defender: So? So that's the difference. The victims of criminal force are innocent, but the victims of the force used by the criminal justice system are not at all innocent. So even if the system functions unjustly or ineffectively, as long as it uses force against people who have done wrong, it is morally different from crime. Suppose you're right that the system punishes some killers and not others. *We* may think it is unjust that the poor guy who shoots his neighbor goes to prison, while the executive responsible for deadly occupational hazards goes free. But that poor murderer can't complain. *He* can't cry injustice, since, after all, he did kill someone and deserves punishment regardless of what happens to anyone else. I think this is why the criminal justice system may be accused of exercising force unjustly *but not criminally*—this is why I think your argument rests on a confusion. The system may be unjust and it may be ineffective in protecting us, but the objects of its force are not innocent victims. This is the moral difference between the criminal justice system and criminality.

Critic: I admit that some of the "victims" of the criminal justice system get what they deserve. But I think it is a mistake to think that the only victims of criminal justice policy are the people who get locked up. The criminal justice system is responsible for the victims of the acts that it doesn't use force to prevent. Since it is *the* institution that uses force to prohibit harmful acts, what it doesn't prohibit, *it permits*. Indeed, since it is the *only* institution allowed to use force, what it permits, *it protects*. The criminal justice system has many victims, and most of them are clearly innocent.

Defender: Who are the innocent victims of criminal justice?

Critic: Well, first, and least controversially, there are the *millions* of citizens who fork over more than $12 billion a year (on pain of imprisonment) in taxes to pay for the false illusion of protection and justice. *This is robbery in the name of criminal justice.* Then there are the hundreds of thousands of citizens who are killed or injured by safety hazards and all the other acts that the system either winks at or closes its eyes to entirely. These people are victimized not merely because the system neglects to use force to protect them but even more so because the system uses force to protect the wealth and power of those who harm them. Add to them the thousands who are victimized by the crimes of heroin addicts and of ex-convicts who can't get a decent job and by the crimes that are facilitated and intensified by the availability of guns. *This is a whole FBI Index of property "crimes" and violent "crimes" that result from criminal justice policy.* And the victims are innocent.

Defender: And the other victims?

Critic: The others are not uncontrovertably innocent, but neither are they clearly guilty. These are all those who are either punished or live in fear of punishment for *victimless crimes*, that is, for acts that harm no one. Those who are punished for using marijuana or heroin, for prostitution or homosexual behavior and the like are innocent victims of the criminal justice system.

Defender: And what of those who are punished for crimes with victims, are they also innocent "victims" of criminal justice?

Critic: I would say that for many of them, their moral guilt is questionable, and to that extent they are victimized by the system.

Defender: Before, you said that you believe that most of those now serving jail or prison sentences are guilty of the crimes for which they were convicted.

Critic: I believe that most are *legally* guilty. I think the extent of their *moral* guilt is questionable. So many of those in our prisons are poor that it seems reasonable to doubt that they would have committed the crimes that got them in prison if they had not suffered the disabilities and disadvantages of poverty. If this is so, who is morally responsible for the crimes of the poor? The poor who didn't choose their poverty or the affluent who choose to do little or nothing to rectify it? We've seen that there is reason to believe that a society like ours provokes crime in all economic classes, although most intensely in the lowest classes. If this is so, can you be so sure that the criminals punished by the system are not in a more profound sense really innocent victims of the system, at least in the sense that they are not morally responsible for the social conditions that have made crime such a reasonable and tempting option for them?[2]

Defender: I think you are being a bit maudlin about criminals. Many of them are pretty nasty, not at all as innocent as you picture them.

Critic: I knew you would say that. But I have no illusions about those criminals. I don't doubt that many are dangerous and nasty and that we need to be protected against them. This, however, shouldn't be used as an excuse for ignoring the social sources of their nastiness. And if those sources are to be found in the poverty our society allows, in the selfishness our society encourages, and in the institutions our criminal justice system protects, then there is a profound sense in which our criminals are our victims. And the punishment we heap upon them is just a continuation of the pains we have allowed them to suffer since birth, for no fault of their own.

Defender: Poverty is no excuse for hurting other people—certainly not other poor people.

Critic: Look, I agree with you. My point is not that all criminals are innocent. But rather that for many, their moral guilt is less because of the social conditions in which they exist. They may well be morally guilty of their crimes in part—but for many, there is reason to believe that their guilt is at least shared by the society that allows crime-producing conditions to flourish. My point is that if you add to these all the victims of the system's action and inaction who are clearly innocent, the inescapable conclusion is that of all the hundreds of thousands of victims of our criminal justice policies and practices, many are clearly innocent, many are of questionable guilt, and a small fraction of the total are really getting what they deserve. *This is enough, I think, to make the case that the criminal justice system is morally no better than crime.* That the system is more *criminal* than *just.*

At this point the dialogue breaks off.

---

b. Rehabilitating Criminal Justice in America

The criminal justice system in America is morally indistinguishable from criminality because it exercises force and imposes suffering on human beings *while violating its own morally justifying ideals: protection and justice.* Once this is understood, the requirements for rehabilitating the system follow rather directly. The system must do those things that make good on its claim to protect society and to do justice. In the remainder of this chapter I will briefly suggest the outlines of a "treatment strategy" for *helping the system go straight.* It cannot be reiterated too frequently that these proposals are not offered as a means of *improving* the system. They are presented as the necessary requirements for establishing the criminal justice system's moral difference from, and moral superiority to, *crime.* The proposals fall under the headings of the two ideals that justify the existence of a criminal justice system. These ideals require that the criminal justice system protect us against the real dangers that threaten us and that it not be an accomplice to injustice in the larger society. In order to realize these ideals, it is necessary that the harms and injustices done by the criminal justice system itself be eliminated.

1. Protecting Society

First, it must be acknowledged that every day that we refuse to implement those strategies that have a good chance of cutting down on the crimes people fear—the crimes on the FBI Index—the system is an accomplice to these crimes and bears responsibility for the suffering they impose.

• *We must enact and vigorously enforce stringent gun controls.*

Americans are armed to the teeth. The handgun is the most easily concealed, the most effective, and the deadliest weapon there is. Its ubiquity is a constant temptation to would-be crooks who lack the courage or skill to commit crimes without weapons or to chance hand-to-hand combat. Its ubiquity also means that any dispute may be transformed into a fatal conflict beyond the desires or expectations of the disputants. Trying to fight crime while allowing America to remain an armed camp is like trying to teach a child to walk and tripping him each time he stands up. In its most charitable light, it is hypocrisy. Less charitably, it is complicity in murder.[3]

- *We must legalize the production and sale of heroin and treat addiction as a medical problem.*

Although most observers seem to agree that the British system of dispensing heroin to registered addicts is superior to our own punitive system, a number of experts have gone even further. Norval Morris and Gordon Hawkins urge that narcotics use be decriminalized and that drugs be sold in pharmacies by prescription. Philip Baridon recommends that pure heroin—clearly labeled as to contents, recommended dosage, and addictive potential—be sold at a low fixed price in pharmacies, without prescription, to anyone aged 18 or over.[4] I shall not enter into debate about the various ways in which heroin can be decriminalized. I make the simple point that when heroin addicts cannot obtain heroin legally, they will obtain it illegally. And since those who sell it illegally have a captive market, they will charge high prices to make their own risks worthwhile. To pay the high prices, addicts must and will and do resort to crime. Thus, every day in which we keep the acquisition of heroin a crime, we are using the law to protect the high profits of heroin black marketeers, *and* we are creating a situation in which large numbers of individuals are virtually physically compelled to commit theft. Since there is little evidence that heroin is dangerous beyond the fact of addiction itself, there can be little doubt that our present "cure" for narcotics use is more criminal (and criminogenic) than the narcotics themselves.

- *We must develop correctional programs that promote rather than undermine personal responsibility, and we*

must offer ex-offenders real preparation and a real oppor-
tunity to make it as law-abiding citizens.

The scandal of our prisons has been amply documented.
Like our attitudes toward guns and heroin, they seem more
calculated to produce than reduce crime. The enforced
childhood of imprisonment may be the painful penalty
offenders deserve, but if it undermines their capacity to go
straight after release, we are cutting off our noses to spite our
faces. People cannot learn to control themselves responsibly
if they have spent years having every minute of their lives—
the hour they wake, the number of minutes they wash, the
time and content of eating and working and exercising, the
hour at which lights go out—regulated by someone else. Add
to this the fact that convicts usually emerge with no marketable skill and little chance of getting a decent job with the
stigma of a prison sentence hanging over them. The result is
a system in which we never let criminals finish paying their
debt to society and give them every incentive to return to
crime.

If we are going to continue to punish people by depriving
them of their liberty, we must do it in a way that prepares
them for the life they will lead when their liberty is returned.
Anything less than this is a violation of the Constitution's
Eighth Amendment guarantee against "cruel and unusual
punishment." Depriving a person of his or her liberty may be
an acceptable punishment, but *depriving people of their
dignity and a chance to live a law-abiding life when their
punishment is supposed to be over is cruel and* (should be, but
sadly is not) *unusual!*

Pursuant to this Eighth Amendment guarantee, every
imprisoned person should have a right to training at a
marketable skill as well as a right to compete equally with
non-ex-convicts for a job once the punishment is over. This
would require that it be illegal to discriminate against
ex-convicts in hiring and illegal to require job applicants to
state whether or not they had ever been arrested, convicted,
and/or imprisoned for a crime. This might have to be

modified for particularly sensitive occupations, although on the whole I think it would be fairer and more effective in rehabilitating ex-cons to enact it across the board and to have the government finance or subsidize a fund to ensure against losses incurred as a result of ex-convicts. My hunch is that this would be much less costly than paying to support ex-cons in prison and their families on welfare when they return to crime for lack of a job. Beyond this, prison industries should pay inmates at prevailing wages; this money then could be used for restitution to victims and to purchase privileges and possibly increased privacy or freedom for the prisoners—all of which might tend to give them greater practice at controlling their own lives so that they will be prepared to do so after release.

But none of this will give us a criminal justice system worthy of the name, until we:

- *Let the crime fit the harm and the punishment fit the crime.*

For the criminal justice system to justify it methods, it must make good on its claim to protect society. This requires that the criminal law be redrawn so that the list of crimes reflects the real dangers that individuals pose to society. Avoidable acts where the actor had reason to know that his or her acts were likely to lead to someone's death should be counted as forms of murder. Avoidable acts where the actor had reason to believe that his or her acts were likely to lead to someone's injury should be counted as forms of assault and battery. And acts that illegitimately deprive people of their money or possessions should be treated as forms of theft regardless of whether the thief's collar is white or colored. Crime in the suites should be prosecuted and punished as vigorously as crime in the streets.

The law must be drawn carefully so that individuals are not punished for harm they could not foresee or could not have avoided and so that the pursuit of security does not swamp the legitimate claims of liberty. However, within

these guidelines, we must rid the law of the distinction
between *one-on-one* harm and *indirect* harm *and treat all
harm-producing acts in proportion to the actual harm they
produce.*[5] *We must enact and implement punishments that
fit the harmfulness of the crime without respect to the class of
the criminal.* There is, for instance, general agreement that
incarceration functions as an effective deterrent to corporate
crime where the threat of imprisonment is believed.[6] And to
be believed, it must be used.

The other side of this coin is the decriminalization of
"victimless crimes," acts such as prostitution, homosexuality, gambling, vagrancy, drunkenness, and of course,
drug use. As long as these acts only involve persons who
have freely chosen to participate, they represent no threat to
the liberty of any citizen. But this also means that there is
generally no complainant for these crimes, no person who
feels harmed by these acts and who is ready and able to press
charges and testify against the wrongdoers. Therefore,
police have to use a variety of shady and suspect tactics
involving deception and bordering on entrapment, which
undermine the public's respect for the police and the police
officers' respect for themselves. In any event, the use of such
low-visibility tactics increases the likelihood of corruption
and arbitrariness in the enforcement of the law. Beyond this,
since these acts produce no palpable, undeniable, tangible
harm, laws against them appear to be no more than the
impositon of some people's ideas of virtue on others, rather
than laws that really protect society. To make good on its
claim to protect society, the criminal justice system must not
only treat the dangerous acts of business executives as
crimes, but it must also decriminalize those acts that are not
clearly dangerous.[7]

Over 100 years ago, John Stuart Mill formulated what has
stood the test of time as the guiding principle for the design of
legislation in a society committed to personal liberty:

That principle is, that the sole end for which mankind are
warranted, individually or collectively, in interfering with the

liberty of action of any of their number, is self-protection. That
the only purpose for which power can be rightfully exerised
over any member of a civilized community, against his will, is
to prevent harm to others.[8]

Although the principle has had to be modified in recognition
of the ways in which individuals can cause future harm to
themselves because of present injudicious choices, particularly in a complex modern society where people must deal
with machines and chemicals beyond their understanding,[9]
the heart of the principle is still widely accepted. This is the
notion that a necessary condition of any justifiable legal
prohibition is that it prohibit an act that does harm to
someone, possibly the actor himself. Since presumption
should be given to freedom of action, this harm should be
demonstrable (i.e., detectable by some widely agreed upon
means, say, those used by medical science), and it should be
of sufficient gravity to outweigh the value of the freedom that
is to be legally prohibited.[10]

This principle should not only guide legislators and those
engaged in revising and codifying criminal law, but it should
be raised to the level of an implicit Constitutional principle.
The U.S. Supreme Court recognizes certain traditional principles of legality as Constitutional requirements even though
they are not explicitly written into the Constitution. For
instance, some laws have been held unconstitutional because
of their vagueness[11] and others because they penalized a
condition (like being a drunk or an addict) rather than an
action (like drinking or using drugs).[12] It strikes me that the
entire tenor of the Bill of Rights is to enshrine and protect
individual liberty from the encroachment of the state. But
legal philosophers from Mill to the present have argued that
to give priority to individual liberty, one must accept some
version of the demonstrable harm requirement as a condition
for acceptable laws. This is because an act that threatens no
harm is no threat to liberty, so a law that prohibits such an
act is a limitation on liberty with no counterbalancing gain
in liberty to justify it. In this light, it seems reasonable that

the Supreme Court should strike down as *unconstitutional* any criminal law that prohibits an act that does not cause demonstrable harm, with the burden of proof lying with the state to demonstrate the palpable harm the law seeks to prevent.

Whether as a legislative or a judicial criterion, however, this principle would undoubtedly rid our law of the excrescences of our puritan moralism. It would bring our law more in line with a realistic view of what is harmful, and it would eliminate the forced induction into criminality of the individuals—mainly those of the lower class—who get arrested for "victimless crimes."

These changes, taken together, would be likely to reduce dangerous crime and to bring us a legal order that actually punished (and, it is hoped, deterred) all and only those acts that really threaten our lives and possessions and punished them in proportion to the harm they really produce. Such a legal system could be truly said to protect society.

2. Promoting Justice

The changes recommended above would go some considerable distance toward making the criminal justice system more just, since people would be punished in proportion to the seriousness of their antisocial acts, and the number of innocent persons victimized by those acts would be reduced. Much would still remain to be done to eliminate the disabilities of the poor caught up in the system.

A criminal justice system should arrest, charge, convict, and sentence individuals with an eye only to their crime, not to their class. Any evidence of more frequent arrest or harsher penalties for poor persons than for others accused of the same crime is a grave injustice that tends to undermine the legitimacy of the criminal justice system. Since many of the decisions that work to the disadvantage of the poor— police decisions to arrest, prosecutors' decisions to charge, and judges' decisions on how long to sentence—are exercises of discretion often out of public view, they are particularly resistant to control. Since, unlike prosecutors' or judges' decisions, the police officer's decision *not* to arrest is *not* a matter of record, it is the least visible exercise of discretion and the most difficult to control. Our best hope to make it more just lies in increased citizen awareness and education of police officers so that they at least become aware of the operation and impact of their own biases and are held more directly accountable to, and by, the public they serve and sometimes arrest.

As for prosecutorial and judicial discretion, two approaches seem potentially fruitful. First, our lawmakers ought to spell out the acceptable criteria that prosecutors may use in deciding whether or what to charge and the criteria that judges may use in deciding whether or what to sentence. The practice of multiple charging (e.g., charging an accused burglar with "the lesser included crimes" of breaking and entering, possession of burglar's tools, etc.) should be eliminated. It is used by prosecutors to "coax" accused persons into pleading guilty to one charge by threatening to press *all* charges. Of all the dubious features of our system of bargain justice, this seems most clearly without justification, since it works to coerce a plea of guilty which should be uncoerced if it is to be legally valid.[13] The law should also set out more specific sentencing ranges, since the present system leads to individuals receiving wildly different sentences for the same crimes—a practice that can only be viewed as arbitrary and capricious, that violates the principle that citizens should know in advance what is in store for them if they break a law, and that produces in convicts disrespect for the law rather than remorse for their violations. In addition to, and in conjunction with, these legislative changes, we ought to require prosecutors and judges to put in writing the reasons they have charged or sentenced in one way rather than another. And they should be required to give an account of their policies and practices to some truly representative body to show that they are fair and reasonable. However we achieve it, it is clear that to make the criminal justice system function justly:

- *We must narrow the range in which police officers, prose-cutors and judges exercise discretion, and we must de-velop procedures to hold them all accountable to the public for the fairness and reasonableness of their decisions.*

But all these changes still leave standing what is probably the largest source of injustice to the poor in the system: *unequal access to quality legal counsel.* The striking fact about the present inmates of our state correctional facilities is that fully 70 percent could not afford to retain their own private counsel. Since we know that, by and large, privately retained counsel will have more incentive to put in the time and effort to get their clients off the hook, and since we know that this results in a situation in which *for equal crimes* those who can retain their own counsel are more likely to be acquitted than those who cannot, the present system of allocating assigned counsel or public defenders to the poor, and privately retained lawyers to the affluent, is little more than a parody of the Constitutional guarantee of a *right to counsel* and a clear violation of the Constitutional guarantee of *equal protection under the law.*

There are simply no two ways about this. In our system, even though lawyers are assigned to the poor, justice has a price. Those who pay get the choicest cuts—those who cannot, get the scraps. A hundred years or so ago, before there were organized police forces in every town and city, people got "police protection" by hiring private police officers or bodyguards if they could afford it. Protection was avail-able for a price, and so those who had more money were better protected under the law. Today, we regard it as every citizen's right to have police protection, and we would find it outrageous if police protection were allocated to citizens on a fee-for-service basis. *But this is precisely where we stand with respect to the legal protection provided by lawyers!*

Legal protection is not only provided by the police. Attorneys are necessary to protect individuals from losing their freedom at the hands of the law before they have exhausted the legal defenses that are theirs by right. Both police officers and lawyers are essential to the individual's legal protection. It is sheer hypocrisy to acknowledge everyone's right to equal protection under the law by the police and then to allocate protection under the law by lawyers on the basis of what individuals can pay. As long as this continues, we cannot claim that there is anything like equal treatment before the law in the criminal justice system.

- *We must transform the equal right to counsel into the right to equal counsel, as far as it is possible.*

Although this would appear to be a clear requirement of the "equal protection" and "due process" clauses of the Constitution, the Supreme Court has avoided it, perhaps because it poses massive practical problems. And surely it does. However, organized police forces to protect everyone probably seemed a massive tangle of practical problems in their time as well.

Certainly it would not be appropriate to use the police as a model for resolving the problem of equal counsel. To establish a governmental legal service for all—in effect to nationalize the legal profession—might make equal legal representation available to all. It would, however, undermine the adversary system by undercutting the independence of the defense attorney from the state. Some form of national legal insurance to enable all individuals to hire private attorneys of their own choice, however, could bring us closer to equal legal protection without compromising the adversarial relationship.

Such a system would undoubtedly have to be subsidized by the government, as are the police and the courts and prisons, but it would not necessarily have to be totally paid for out of taxes. People might rightly be expected to pay their legal bills up to some fraction of their income, if they have one. The rest would be paid for by a government subsidy which would pay the difference between what the accused could afford and the going rate for high-quality legal counsel. Nothing in the system need interfere with the freedom of the accused to select the lawyer of his or her choice (an option closer to the hearts of free enterprisers than the present public defender system allows) or interfere with the independence of the lawyer.

Undoubtedly, such a system would be costly. But our commitment to equal justice remains a sham until we are willing to pay this price. Americans have paid dearly to protect the value of liberty enshrined in the Constitution—is it too much to expect that they will pay to realize the ideal of justice enshrined there too?

One final recommendation remains to be made. I have already argued that the criminal justice system, by its very nature, embodies the prevailing economic relations in its laws. This means that it is an error to think of the criminal justice system as an entity that can be reformed in isolation from the larger social order. A criminal justice system is a means to protect that social order, and it can be no more just than the order it protects. A law against theft may be enforced with an even and just hand. But if it protects an unjust distribution of wealth and property, the result is *injustice evenly enforced.* A criminal justice system cannot hold individuals guilty of the injustice of breaking the law if the law itself supports and defends an unjust social order.

- *We must establish a more just distribution of wealth and income and make equal opportunity a reality for all Americans.*

This is not a proposal *added on* to my prescriptions for rehabilitating criminal justice—it is one of those prescriptions. Without economic and social justice, the police officer in the ghetto is indeed an occupying soldier with no more legitimacy than his or her gun provides. Without economic and social justice the criminal justice system is the defender of injustice and is thus morally indistinguishable from the criminal. *A criminal justice system can be no more just than the society its laws protect.* Along with the other recommendations I have made in this chapter, the achievement of economic and social justice is a necessary condition for establishing the criminal justice system's moral difference from, and moral superiority to, *crime*.

* * *

Every step toward domestic disarmament, toward decriminalization of heroin and "victimless crimes," toward criminalization of the dangerous acts of the affluent and vigorous prosecution of "white-collar" crimes; every step toward creating a correctional system that promotes human dignity, toward giving ex-offenders a real opportunity to go straight, toward making the exercise of power by police officers, prosecutors, and judges more reasonable and more just, toward giving all individuals accused of crime equal access to high-quality legal expertise in their defense; every step toward establishing economic and social justice is a step that moves us from a system of *criminal* justice to a system of criminal *justice*. The refusal to take those steps is a move in the opposite direction.

Footnotes

1. Although I think this way of looking at the legal system, at justice, and at the moral legitimacy of the law, is common to most moral and legal philosophers, it should be acknowledged that my own formulation bears a heavy debt to the conceptions of justice and morality developed by John Rawls, Kurt Baier, and Herbert Morris. See John Rawls, *A Theory of Justice* (Cambridge, Mass.: Harvard University Press, 1971); Kurt Baier, *The Moral Point of View: A Rational Basis of Ethics* (New York: Random House, 1965); and Herbert Morris, "Persons and Punishment," in A. I. Melden, ed., *Human Rights* (Belmont, California: Wadsworth, 1970), pp. 111-134. On the

issue of the legitimacy of states (i.e., political-legal systems),
see Robert Paul Wolff, *In Defense of Anarchism* (New York:
Harper & Row, 1970 and 1976), Jeffrey H. Reiman, *In Defense
of Political Philosophy* (New York: Harper & Row, 1972),
Reiman, "Autonomy, Authority, and Universalizability," in
The Personalist (January, 1978), pp. 85-92; and Reiman "Anarchism and Nominalism: Wolff's Latest Obituary for Political Philosophy," in *Ethics* (October, 1978). On the issue of the
legitimacy and moral justification of police authority in particular, see Jeffrey H. Reiman, "Police Autonomy vs. Police
Authority: A Philosophical Perspective," in *The Police Community*, eds., Jack Goldsmith and Sharon S. Goldsmith (Pacific Palisades, Calif.: Palisades Publishers, 1974), pp. 225-233;
and Roger Wertheimer, "Are the Police Necessary?," in *The
Police in Society*, eds., Emilio C. Viano and Jeffrey H. Reiman,
(Lexington, Mass.: Lexington Books, 1975), pp. 49-60.

2. This is an important point both practically and theoretically.
Moral guilt for breaking a law does not arise in a vacuum.
One's moral guilt for breaking a law is only as great as one's
moral obligation to comply with it. Contemporary moral
philosophers generally maintain that one's moral obligation
to comply with laws is a function of the benefits one receives
from the social order that the legal system protects and makes
possible. The social contract metaphor certainly suggests
this, since a contract has at least two sides. One is bound to
fulfill his or her part of a contract to the extent that the other
parties to the contract fulfill theirs. If we conceive of the
obligation to obey the laws as each individual's obligation to
do his or her part in the social contract, then quite clearly
one's obligation is only strong to the extent that one's own
contribution to the contract is matched with contributions by
the others which are commensurate in value. In short, this
means that one is obligated if the terms of the contract are
fair and if everyone, on the whole, is also keeping their part
of the bargain. Arguing from such a framework, John Rawls
concludes that "the duty to comply is problematic for per-
manent minorities that have suffered from injustice for many
years." *A Theory of Justice*, p. 355. Applying Rawl's theory
to the question of the obligation of deprived minorities to obey
laws which result in economic injustice towards them, Phillip
H. Scribner maintains that "just as we are not obligated to
acquiesce in the denial of our basic liberties, we are not

required to cooperate in our own exploitation." "On the Duty
to Obey an Unjust Law," in *The Police in Society*, eds., Viano
and Reiman, p. 43. Michael Walzer, treating the subject from a
somewhat different perspective, concludes that "the oppressed
do not receive all the . . . benefits [of the political community]
because they are not counted equally. They are in a special
and very difficult position that may best be defined by
suggesting that they possess within the state the liberty to
refuse, to say no to the laws they have not been able to join
in making. They possess the liberty to refuse because they
have themselves been refused full participation in the democratic community." "The Obligations of Oppressed Minorities," in *Obligations: Essays on Disobedience, War and Citizenship* (New York: Simon and Schuster, 1970), p. 69. All this
adds up to one conclusion: *The obligation to obey the law is
decreased when one is on the receiving end of injustice, and
therefore the moral guilt for disobeying the law must decrease
as well.*

3. See the thoughtful recommendations for gun control and their
    rationale in Norval Morris and Gordon Hawkins, *The Honest
    Politician's Guide to Crime Control* (Chicago: University of
    Chicago Press, 1970), pp. 63-71.

4. Morris and Hawkins, pp. 3, and 8-10; and Philip C. Baridon,
    Addiction, Crime, and Social Policy (Lexington, Mass.: Lex-
    ington Books, 1976), p. 88.

5. For a convincing argument that there is no moral difference
    between directly caused and indirectly caused harm, see John
    Harris, "The Marxist Conception of Violence," *Philosophy &
    Public Affairs*, 3, No. 2 (winter, 1974), pp. 192-220; and
    Jonathan Glover, *Causing Death and Saving Lives* (Ham-
    mondsworth, England: Penguin, 1977), pp. 92-112.

6. These are the words of a former director of the fraud division
    of the Department of Justice: "No one in direct contact with the
    living reality of business conduct in the United States is
    unaware of the effect the imprisonment of seven high officials
    in the Electrical Machinery Industry in 1960 had on the con-
    spiratorial price fixing in many areas of our economy; similar
    sentences in a few cases each decade would almost completely
    cleanse our economy of the cancer of collusive price fixing and
    the mere prospect of such sentences is itself the strongest
    available deterrent to such activities." Gordon B. Spivak,
    "Antitrust Enforcement in the United States: A Primer,"

Connecticut Bar Journal, 37 (September, 1963), p. 382.

7.   See Chapter One, "The Overreach of the Criminal Law," in Morris and Hawkins, pp. 1-28; Herbert Packer, *The Limits of the Criminal Sanction* (Stanford, Calif.: Stanford University Press, 1968); and Jeffrey H. Reiman, "Can We Avoid the Legislation of Morality?," in *Legality, Morality and Ethics in Criminal Justice*, eds., Nicholas N. Kittrie and Jackwell Susman (New York: Praeger, forthcoming).

8.   John Stuart Mill, *On Liberty* (1859), (New York: Appleton-Century Crofts, 1947), p. 9.

9.   See, for example, Gerald Dworkin, "Paternalism," in *Morality and the Law*, ed., Richard Wasserstrom (Belmont, Calif.: Wadsworth, 1971), pp. 107-126; and Joel Feinberg, "Legal Paternalism," in *Today's Moral Problems*, ed., Richard Wasserstrom (New York: Macmillan, 1975), pp. 33-50.

10.   See, for instance, the excellent discussion of the principle in Peter T. Manicas, *The Death of the State* (New York: Putnam, 1974), Chapter V: "The Liberal Moral Ideal," pp. 194-241; and H. L. A. Hart, *Law, Liberty and Morality* (New York: Vintage Books, 1963).

11.   The standard laid down in *Conally v. General Constr. Co.*, 269 U.S. 385, 391, 70 L. Ed. 322, 46 S. Ct. 126 (1926) is "whether or not the vagueness is of such a character 'that men of common intelligence must necessarily guess at its meaning.'" See also *Lanzetta et al. v. State of New Jersey*, 306, U.S. 451, 83 L. Ed. 888, 59 S. Ct. 618 (1939), where the Supreme Court struck down a New Jersey statute that made it a felony for anyone not engaged in any lawful occupation to be a member of a gang, etc., because the terms of the statute were "vague, indefinite and uncertain" and thus "repugnant to the due process clause of the Fourteenth Amendment." Both cases are cited and discussed in Jerome Hall, *General Principles of Criminal Law*, 2nd edition (New York: Bobbs-Merrill, 1960), pp. 36-48.

12.   See *Robinson* v. *California*, 370 U.S. 66 (1962), where the court held that a state law penalizing a person for a "status" such as addiction constitutes "cruel and unusual punishment" in violation of the Eighth Amendment. Cited and discussed in Nicholas N. Kittrie, *The Right to be Different: Deviance and Enforced Therapy* (Baltimore: The Johns Hopkins Press, 1971), pp. 35-36, inter alia.

13. I have already pointed out that the vast majority of persons
convicted of crimes in the United States are not convicted by
juries. They plead guilty as the result of a "bargain" with
the prosecutor (underwritten by the judge), in which the prosecutor agrees to drop other charges in return for the guilty plea.
Kenneth Kipnis argues that the entire system of bargain
justice is a violation of the ideal of justice, since it amounts
to coercing a guilty plea and often to punishing an offender for
a crime other than the one he or she has committed. It is an
argument worth considering. See Kenneth Kipnis, "Criminal
Justice and the Negotiated Plea," *Ethics*, 86, No. 2 (January,
1976), pp. 93-106.

Index